Southwest Florida's Plan to Combat Terrorism

Southwest Florida's Plan to Combat Terrorism

✦

An Interdisciplinary Perspective

An Interdisciplinary Case Study

Dr. Judith Kolva, Zaida Brown, Cindy Burnett, Carla Cavero, Jodi A. Figueroa, Barb Giacalione, Claude Lordeus, Steve Martin, Lisa Mead, Joe Norris, Steve S. Perkins, Sr., Rick Torres, D'Arcy Tuyls, Thom Ward

International College, Naples and Ft. Myers, Florida

www.internationalcollege.edu

iUniverse, Inc.
New York Lincoln Shanghai

Southwest Florida's Plan to Combat Terrorism
An Interdisciplinary Perspective

iUniverse books may be ordered through booksellers or by contacting:

iUniverse
2021 Pine Lake Road, Suite 100
Lincoln, NE 68512
www.iuniverse.com
1-800-Authors (1-800-288-4677)

ISBN-13: 978-0-595-40404-9 (pbk)
ISBN-13: 978-0-595-84779-2 (ebk)
ISBN-10: 0-595-40404-9 (pbk)
ISBN-10: 0-595-84779-X (ebk)

Printed in the United States of America

Contents

Acknowledgments

"Guard well within yourself that treasure, kindness. Know how to give without hesitation, how to lose without regret, how to acquire without meanness."

—George Sand (1804–1876)

We gratefully acknowledge all of those who helped us on our journey.

Marilyn Benson, International College

Dr. Ron Bowman, International College

Cpl. Bob Brown, Collier County Deputy

Skip Camp

Lori Cohen, Temple Shalom

Cl. Terry Coker and the Gulf Coast High School Junior ROTC

Mel Fisher, Bonita Springs Water and Waste Utilities, Inc.

Joe Frazier, Collier County Emergency Management

Susan Gallen, Executive Assistant to Governor Ridge

J. Dudley Goodlette, Florida House of Representatives

Jamie Hardesty, International College

Elsie Hillman

Don Hunter, Collier County Sheriff

International College Staff and Faculty

Patrick Kayhearst

John Kepsel, Temple Shalom

Lt. Bruno Lovo, paramedic

Michael McNerney, Lee County Schools

Ed Messer, Collier County Schools

Bill Moyer, Battalion Chief

Kevin Nelms, fireman/paramedic

Lt. Commander Chris O'Neil, Coast Guard

Governor Tom Ridge, Former Director of Homeland Security

Dr. Elsa Rogers, International College

Greg Spears

Dan Summers, Collier County Emergency Management

John Varsames, Naples Civil Air Patrol

> *"When I heard this was a group of interdisciplinary studies students, I had to get involved. Nothing was more interdisciplinary than the creation of the Department where we put 128 entities under one umbrella."*
>
> —*Tom Ridge, Former Director of Homeland Security.*

About the Authors

Dr. Judith Kolva—*You can not discover new oceans unless you have courage to lose sight of the shore.*

Dr. Kolva holds a doctorate of philosophy in psychology. She is a professor and personal historian. Her hobbies include jazz, SCUBA, reading, and writing.

Zaida Brown—*Do unto others as you would have them do unto you—Internal beauty is the manifestation of the divine.*

Zaida is pursuing a bachelor's degree in interdisciplinary studies. She hopes to some day teach Spanish and work with gifted children. Her hobbies include reading, dancing, swimming and spending time at the gym.

Cindy Burnett—*People will forget what you said; people will forget what you did, but people will not forget how you made them feel.*

Cindy is pursuing her bachelor's degree in interdisciplinary studies. In the immediate future she wants to spend more time with her children.

Carla Cavero—*Emotional intelligence is the key to success.*

Carla is pursuing her bachelor's degree in interdisciplinary studies with a minor in psychology. She intends to continue her education toward a master's degree in business. She owns a growing construction company and expects to continue in that endeavor. Her hobbies include writing poetry, swimming and dancing.

Jodi Figueroa—*Love all people; there is only one race, the human race.*

Jodi is pursuing her bachelor's degree in interdisciplinary studies with a minor in psychology. She intends to continue her education toward a master's degree in counseling and someday work as a crisis and bereavement counselor. Her hobbies include ice hockey and open water diving.

Barbara Giacalione—*Fortuna Favet Audentes.*

Barb is pursuing her bachelor's degree in interdisciplinary studies. Barb plans to move forward with environmental studies. She is a health department professional. Her hobby is her special interest in the history of Mythology.

Claude Lordeus—*Don't say too much, you will survive.*

Claude is pursuing his bachelor's degree in interdisciplinary studies. He plans to continue his studies in the field of computer science. His future plan is to work in law enforcement. His hobbies include auto racing and traveling.

Steve Martin—*Determination is a powerful tool.*

Steve is pursuing his bachelor's degree in interdisciplinary studies. He plans on continuing his teaching career. His special interest areas are math and science. Along with his love for athletics he would like to be a coach. His hobbies include cycling, baseball and making watches.

Lisa Mead—*For Kyle and Katie—to show them the power of believing in yourself.*

Lisa is pursuing her bachelor's degree in interdisciplinary studies. She intends to continue her education and obtain a doctorate of philosophy in teaching. Her goal is to become a professor. Her hobbies include water sports, cooking and reading.

Joe Norris—*Treat everyone the same.*

Joe is pursuing his bachelor's degree in interdisciplinary studies. He plans to continue his education in the fields of math, English and psychology. He hopes to teach 8th/9th grade science. His hobbies include reading science books and exploring photography.

Steven S. Perkins, Sr.—*Courage is resistance to fear, mastery of fear not absence of fear.*

Steve is pursuing his bachelor's degree in interdisciplinary studies. He plans to pursue a career in teaching and writing. His hobbies include watching, playing and coaching hockey.

Rolando "Rick" Torres—*Semper fidelis.*

Rick is pursuing his bachelor's degree in interdisciplinary studies. He plans to earn a master's degree in public administration. As a current employee of Collier County, he wishes to obtain a position in management. His hobbies include running, fishing and reading.

D'Arcy Tuyls—For *Marni…live, love, laugh and always learn.*

D'Arcy is pursuing her bachelor's degree in interdisciplinary studies. She plans to earn a master's degree in special education and teach special needs children. She enjoys spending quality time with her daughter.

Thom Ward—*When you're green your growing, when you're ripe, you rot.*

Tom is pursuing his bachelor's degree in interdisciplinary studies. He plans to earn a master's degree in psychology and pursue a career as a mental health counselor. His hobbies include reading, cooking and dancing.

Prologue

"Commitment, Character, Community"

—J. Dudley Goodlette
Florida House of Representatives, District 76

We, the authors of this case study, began with a clear vision and mission: We recognize that globalization shrinks our world. Geography no longer dictates our boundaries. The oceans of the world no longer shield us from each other. We spill out of our borders to embrace issues never before encountered. We are pioneers in a yet unexplored paradigm.

Regardless of gender, ethnicity or nationality, the over six billion people on our planet are swarmed daily with the sting of insecurity. Wars, terrorist attacks, civil strife, and religious conflicts besiege us and wound our demand for safety. We pledge to devote our professionalism, expertise, and compassion to this concern. We commit to making solid, proactive decisions that will mold a stable future. We are a unique group of individuals capable of confronting the challenges of the twenty-first century.

We accomplish our mission through the interdisciplinary approach to problem solving. An interdisciplinary paradigm is one in which two or more disciplines are combined in such a way that they interact with and influence each other. Interdisciplinary skills build knowledge and offer solutions that are more inclusive than knowledge and skills shaped in a discipline specific manner. Interdisciplinary solutions offer a rich assimilation of cross discipline concepts and techniques.

Because of our interdisciplinary training, we have the ability to examine complex problems, which in this case relate to homeland security in Southwest Florida, and offer a rich perspective. We understand integration and appreciate individual initiative, ingenuity, self-direction, and cooperation. Through working together, we will create a product of excellence that makes a difference in lives—that contributes to our community.

We recognize challenges develop character, and commit to our mantra:

Action without vision just passes time.
Vision without action is just a dream.
Vision with action can change the world.

Abstract

Undergraduate Interdisciplinary Studies students at International College in Naples, Florida investigated Southwest Florida's plan to combat terrorism. The case study begins with a historical background and psychological perspective on terrorism. It details Southwest Florida's proactive approach to combating terrorism in the areas of immigration, water systems, first responders, preparedness, hospitals, security on the water, surface transportation, airports, temples, and schools. The case study concludes with case questions and a practical application exercise.

Introduction

✦

Southwest Florida's Plan to Combat Terrorism: An Interdisciplinary Perspective

"I don't think we should tell them what we're going to do in advance. Let them think. Worry. Wonder. Uncertainty is the most chilling thing of all."

—*Vernon A. Walters*

―――――――――――――――――――――――――

Consider...

We put our children on the school bus every morning with no thought of how disturbed and angry the young man staring out the window might be. Two hours after arriving on campus, the thin, almost frail, young man is showered and dressed before the howls of laughter stop echoing through the gymnasium. The red and white striped polo shirt and blue jeans he was wearing on the school bus are folded neatly in his gym locker. His white tennis shoes are on the floor of the locker.

These typical high school clothes are replaced with black fatigues, a black T-shirt, and black combat boots. But anyone who knows fashion knows it's the accessories that make the outfit. He dons a black flak-jacket purchased at the Army Surplus Store and slaps together black leather driving gloves stolen from the glove box of his father's BMW. The leather guitar case, concealing the M-15 rifle and three 30 round banana clips, a .45 caliber pistol with four magazines and the sawed off 12 gauge shotgun with two boxes of shells reveal his intentions.

In this case study, you will learn about law enforcement policy changes for engaging an active shooter. You will learn about a new interdisciplinary tech-

1

nique for treating and removing the injured that saves lives in these frightening situations. You will learn about the change in motivations for the terrorist and how law enforcement's shift in paradigms is making our children and teachers safer.

Or perhaps...

Busy, important people move in and out and around the county courthouse like ants on an anthill. Traffic moves about the block unnoticed. The white tractor-trailer truck rounds the corner slowly and pulls up to the side of the courthouse. It is nondescript, lost in the bustle of law-and-order. The driver pulls the truck close to the sidewalk. He ignores the No Parking sign and climbs down from the cab. He joins the crowd on the sidewalk, crosses the street, walks down the next block, turns right at the corner and disappears. No one will remember what he looked like when the investigators are questioning witnesses of the explosion.

In this case study, you will learn about terrorists' favorite means of transportation. You will be reminded of how popular surface transportation is to terrorists and the creative ways they use it. Although securing our infrastructure is difficult, you will learn about the cooperative effort undertaken by the American Trucking Association, American Association of State Highway and Transportation Officials, and the Federal Highway Administration as directed by the Department of Homeland Security.

Or Maybe...

The truck delivering soda to the break rooms inside the water treatment facility arrives about 9:15 a.m., like it does every Tuesday. The driver produces his valid driver's license and magnetic identification card at the security gate. The guard checks the cards against his access list, swipes the ID card through the card reader, smiles at the driver. The driver's property is returned and the guard punches the button that activates the electronic gate.

The driver pulls through the gate with a pleasant, satisfied grin on his face. After backing the truck into the loading dock, the driver loads eight soft drink cases containing a lethal poison on to the hand cart. He then pulls it up the ramp leading to the break room, and dumps the cases into the water treatment tank. He will repeat the process nine more times before driving inconspicuously away.

At 10:45 a.m. Mr. Gavin, an employee of the water treatment facility, is thirsty. He goes to the vending machine and can't believe it is out of grape soda. He could have sworn he saw the Charlton Distributing truck come through the gate at least an hour ago.

A Call to Action…

In this case study, you will learn that is much harder to contaminate the water supply than most people realize. You will learn about proactive safeguards and security measures designed to thwart attempts before any damage is done. You will learn about detection and decontamination procedures that keep us safe even if someone were clever enough to infiltrate a treatment plant. That nagging fear you have about our drinking water will be eliminated.

Terrorist acts, whether committed by domestic terrorists such as troubled teenagers, disgruntled employees, or foreign terrorists looking to disrupt our way of life, are all too common. Since 9/11, hardly a day goes by that we do not hear something about terrorism. Is there anything we can do to protect ourselves? What have our government officials done to make us safer? Are we any safer? It was questions such as these that motivated an undergraduate class of interdisciplinary students at International College in Naples, Florida to seek answers.

Our goal is to answer the questions in a positive, reassuring way. In this case study, you will learn there have been numerous changes, at all governmental levels, aimed at making the populace safer. You will learn about the history of terrorism before 9/11. You will learn about plans for the future, pending legislation, and funding for initiatives. But mostly you will learn about people. You will learn about villains and how they think. You will learn about heroes and heroines and how hard they work to protect their communities.

Another motivation for researching and writing this case study is to inspire readers to seek their own answers. The focus of the study is on Southwest Florida. We hope when you read about what is happening in our region, you will want to find out if your community has implemented safeguards. We urge you to reach out and discover who the people are that hold leadership positions. Who is responsible for your safety? Who is deserving of praise and who won't get your vote next time the polls open? Encourage your community leaders to develop proactive policies against terrorist attacks. From our perspective, it is important for you to take action.

Terrorism in Context

"History is the witness that testifies to the passing of time; it illumines reality, vitalizes memory, provides guidance in daily life and brings us tidings of antiquity."

—*Cicero (106 BC—43 BC)*

Introduction

Attempting to gain an understanding of terrorism is a daunting task. Even recognized experts realize that their comprehension is not complete. O'Day (2004) explains, "Terrorism has a long history stretching from pre-state societies to the present, but scholars have really only begun to uncover and analyze it" (p. 326). To that end, however, we offer the following historical and legal definitions. O'Day describes terrorism as a primitive form of warfare that utilizes elements of ambush and surprise to avoid direct military action. Harmon (2001) gives a colder and more calculated definition of terrorism. He contends, "Terrorism is the deliberate and systematic murder, maiming, and menacing of the innocent to inspire fear for political ends" (p. 1). Florida's legal definition of terrorism, outlined in Florida statute 775.30, considers terrorism any violent act, in violation of the criminal laws of the United States, meant to intimidate the civilian population or influence government policy (*What is Terrorism*, n.d.).

All agree, however, that the face of terrorism is changing. It is becoming more pervasive and more of a threat to society then ever before. Some, such as O'Day (2004), have linked this change to advances in technology, which allow for greater destruction. Huntington (1996), author of *The Clash of Civilizations*, attributes this change to cultural conflicts that have arisen from the globalization of our world's societies. And still others, such as Kegley and Raymond (2005), authors of *The Global Future*, assert that the basic goals of terrorists have changed. Kegley and Raymond say, "Previously, terrorism was regarded as political theater, a frightening drama where the perpetrators wanted a lot of people watching, not a lot of people dead. Now there seemed to be a desire to kill as many people as possible" (p. 169).

Differing viewpoints notwithstanding, terrorism is an issue of fundamental importance in today's world. Researchers and laypeople alike are searching for answers to this enigmatic problem. Perhaps, by studying terrorism's history, that familiarity will produce a greater understanding of today's events.

The Origins of Terrorism

The Roman Empire

One of the first documented instances of terrorism occurred in the first century B.C. when Jewish terrorists incited a revolt against Roman government in Judea. The protestors slaughtered their innocent victims with daggers in open daylight in the center of Jerusalem. This incident created such fear and anxiety among the population that it became the impetus for a mass uprising. The Romans adopted these tactics and for the next 200 years, evoked terror and confusion by massacring humans and animals within the walls of their captured cities (O'Day, 2004).

The Chinese Art of War

Harmon (2001) reports that the handbook on military and psychological warfare, *The Art of War,* written by Sun Tzu in the fourth century B.C. asserts that the purpose of terrorist acts is to create disorder rather than destruction. Within this text, are descriptions of terrorist and guerrilla warfare tactics that Mao Tse Tung adapted and implemented during his reign. These strategies are still wielded by modern-day terrorist groups.

The French Revolution

Some argue that modern terrorism most likely originated during the French Revolution when counter-revolutionaries employed terror tactics against the government of the French Republic. During *The Reign of Terror*, the blade of the guillotine beheaded ordinary citizens and government officials alike. Even royalty, including Marie Antoinette, fell to its swift stroke. Over 30,000 people were killed before the mastermind behind this tactic, Maximilien Robespierre, became its last victim (*Reign of Terror*, 1999).

Terrorism Comes to America

The American Revolution

Before the American Revolution officially began, a group of vigilantes, known as *The Sons of Liberty*, used terror and guerilla tactics to protest British policies. Their goal was to prevent the expansion of British military bases on Colonial soil. This group was so effective that their acts of protest spawned a radical political movement toward independence (O'Day, 2004).

The Civil War

North and South utilized terrorist tactics during the Civil War. General William T. Sherman's raids throughout Georgia and the Carolinas are the best illustration. For ten months, "Sherman intentionally used terrorism in order to cause a steady deterioration of the combat efficiency of homesick Confederate troops" (O'Day, 2004, p. 132). Sherman's forces committed atrocious acts against innocent civilian families. Homes were burned. Belongings were pillaged. Women were raped. Children were slaughtered. After hearing about this devastation, throngs of Southern soldiers deserted the war and returned home. Sherman's violent tactics helped speed the war's end.

Southern Retaliation

Shortly after the Civil War, the Ku Klux Klan (KKK) was founded by Nathan Bedford Forrest and his group of former Confederate soldiers. Their intent was to control the newly freed slaves and transplanted Northerners. The Klan's terrorist acts included cross-burning and lynching. It is estimated that from its inception until the late 1960s, 4,700, mostly African-American people, were lynched by the KKK (*Ku Klux Klan*, 2005). While its influence has waned, effects of the organization's actions are still felt today. Recently, Edgar Ray Killen, ordained minister and KKK member, was convicted of the 1964 manslaughter of three civil rights workers.

America and Modern Terrorism

1993 Bombing of the World Trade Center

On Friday, February 26, 1993 a massive explosion rocked the subterranean garage of the World Trade Center. This blast was meant to cause one of the twin towers to fall onto the other one. In hopes of killing tens of thousands, cyanide gas was to be released. Although six people were killed and over 1,000 were wounded, the terrorists made some serious miscalculations and the more ambitious aims of the attack failed to materialize (Mylroie, 1995). Physical damage from the blast cost upwards of 5 billion dollars, but the psychological damage was even more devastating. In a formal report on the bombing, the Joint Terrorism Task Force (JTTF) declared that, "The sense of fear and panic in the city was palpable" (*The World Trade Center Bombing*, 2005, para. 1).

Shortly after the bombing, four individuals were apprehended and tried in New York City. Each was convicted and sentenced to 240 years in prison. Ramzi Yousef, the man suspected of devising the attack, was captured in 1995 in Pakistan and extradited to the United States. In 1998, Yousef was convicted and sentenced to serve 240 years in prison. Questions regarding the motives and sponsorship of this terrorist faction are still unanswered (*The World Trade Center Bombing*, 2005).

Florida and Terrorist Events

University of South Florida

In 1991, Ramadan Abdullah Shallah became an adjunct professor at the University of South Florida (USF). During his time there he established a think tank called the *World and Islam Studies Enterprise* (WISE). USF and WISE co-sponsored numerous forums on the Middle East. Indeed, the collaboration between the two entities was wide-ranging. USF graduate students were actively involved in WISE programs and members of the think tank were granted access to the university's extensive libraries (Kushner, 1998).

In 1995, Shallah left USF and moved to Syria. Soon after, he was elected to head the Palestinian Islamic Jihad (PIJ), an infamous terrorist organization responsible for more than 100 deaths (Stacy, 2005). The United States froze 12 international fundraising accounts associated with WISE, but the damage had already been done. WISE had raised millions of dollars, obtained Visa's for terrorists to come to the United States and aided the PIJ in their terrorist operations against Israel (Kushner, 1998).

For nearly five years, USF's ties to a terrorist organization went unnoticed by both university officials and the United States government. Mark Orr, the director of USF's International Affairs Center at the time these events took place, concedes that "he and others at the university who embraced the work of the WISE think tank felt betrayed when they learned that Ramadan Abdullah Shallah assumed leadership in 1995 of the PIJ" (Stacy, 2005, para. 3). Today, Shallah and his cohorts face a 53 count indictment for providing material support to a terrorist organization, racketeering and conspiracy.

Training Potential Terrorists

Three of the four terrorists who piloted the hijacked airliners on 9/11 were trained in Venice, Florida. Mohamed Atta, the lead pilot, and Marwan al Shehhi both trained at Huffman Aviation International from July 2000 until they received their licenses in December of that year. The FBI was aware that it was a common practice for Osama Bin Laden to send his minions for flight training in the United States. In fact, ten foreign aviation students were under investigation for ties to Sunni extremists. Unfortunately, on August 7, 2001, the FBI temporarily halted this investigation because they lacked the resources to pursue it (Mitch, 2004).

9/11: A National Tragedy

There are dates that are forever burned into the consciousness of society and 9/11 is one such infamous date. On this day, four commercial airliners were hijacked by 19 terrorists and used as missiles against symbolic civilian targets. Two of the planes crashed into the twin towers of the World Trade Center, causing them to eventually collapse. One of the planes rocketed into the pentagon, causing damage and loss of life. And the fourth plane, intended for another Washington D.C. target, crashed in a field in rural Pennsylvania as passengers valiantly fought to regain control of the plane.

In the end, over three thousand innocent people died (Love, 2003; Stoessinger, 2005). Suddenly Americans were reminded, that absolute evil exists and can change the face of the world. Although the terrorists successfully hit three of their intended targets, their actions had unexpected consequences. Americans emerged from this event determined, resolute and united—just the opposite of what the terrorists sought.

Conclusion

Terrorism has existed since the beginning of recorded history. It has adopted many forms. Some acts, which would today be defined as terrorism, were once considered acts of rebellion for a just cause. And although the acts of modern terrorists have changed in both scope and target, it is clear that these factions feel equally justified in their actions. Understanding this perception on the part of the terrorists is not intended to make one more tolerant of these groups, but does serve to put them into context.

A Psychological Perspective

"The only sin which we never forgive in each other is difference of opinion."

—Ralph Waldo Emerson,
Society and Solitude, 1870

Introduction

The term *psychology* evolves from the root words *psyche*, which means *mind*, and *logos*, which means *study*. Thus, psychology is the study of minds. However, because a mind cannot be seen or touched, psychologists study behaviors (Coon, 2004). It is the discipline of psychology that examines the minds or behaviors of terrorists (Hudson, 1999). Psychologists ask questions such as: What type of person is a terrorist? How does an individual make the decision to participate in terrorist activity? Is there a terrorist mindset, or are terrorists and their groups too diverse to have common psychological traits? In answering these questions, this chapter offers a psychological perspective of a terrorist.

Terrorist Personality Models

Psychologists identify several terrorist personality models. Although each model maintains a separate identity, the end result is the same: Through their actions, terrorists intend to inflict some form of psychological impact on their victims.

The Religious Model

An accurate portrayal of the mindset of the religious terrorist is as follows: Unable to achieve their unrealistic goals by conventional means, international terrorists attempt to send an ideological or religious message by terrorizing the general public. Through the choice of their targets, which are often symbolic or representative of the targeted nation, terrorists attempt to create a high profile impact on the public of their targeted enemy or enemies with their act of violence, despite the limited material resources that are usually at their disposal. In doing so, they hope to demonstrate various points such as that the targeted government(s) cannot protect its (their) own citizens, or that by assassinating a specific victim they can teach the general public a lesson about exposing viewpoints or policies antithetical to their own. (Hudson, 1999, para. 19)

This type of violence has been prevalent in most countries since Roman times. A religious terrorist does not admit that he or she is a terrorist. Instead, he or she claims to be *a freedom fighter* (*Freedom Fighter*, 2005). The psyche of a religious terrorist does not acknowledge his or her actions to be immoral or his or her behavior to be inappropriate. To a religious terrorist, "Terrorism is all about the message" (German, 2005, p. 7).

The Teen Model

Teen terrorists can be separated into two types: 1) those who act out of aggression due to rejection by their peers, and 2) those that are part of a formalized terrorist group such as al-Qaida (Hudson, 1999).

Teen terrorists whose behaviors are the result of peer abuse are usually products of years of being bullied, intimidated and sometimes belittled by their peers. These teens may react with acts of violence toward their peers and teachers. The students who orchestrated the Columbine massacre are an example of this type of terrorist. They were constantly tormented by their peers. During this time, the teens' anger began to compile, yet they remained unnoticed. This type of teen terrorist can be virtually undetectable by authorities because they do not fall into the typical risk categories of terrorists' behaviors.

The second teen model is one of a teen who is a product of his or her environment and religious culture. This terrorist is usually recruited at an early age. They are promised that due to their services, their families will be cared for. These teens believe that joining a terrorist group gives them a sense of "revolutionary heroism and self importance that they previously lacked as individuals" (Hudson, 1999, para. 3.)

The Domestic Model

The definition of domestic terrorism is outlined in the Patriot Act, which reads "Domestic terrorism is limited to conduct that (1) violates federal or state criminal law and (2) is dangerous to human life" ("United States Department of

Justice," n.d.). Timothy McVeigh is an example of an individual considered to be a domestic terrorist. He is infamous for the Oklahoma City bombing. McVeigh was a Persian Gulf War veteran. He was sentenced to death for the Oklahoma bombing that killed 168 people and injured hundreds more. McVeigh was tried under an anti-terrorism law established in 1994 that had not previously been tested before in the United States court system ("McVeigh sentenced to death in federal bombing,"1997). McVeigh displays a perfect example of a domestic terrorist known as a *lone wolf.* Domestic terrorists typically have access to large numbers of people and knowledge about destruction that allows them to commit their horrendous acts. They generally do not attract much attention to themselves and are capable of acts that cause catastrophic damage (Davies, 2005).

The Suicide Model

The suicide terrorist operates on the belief that their actions will produce great consequences and rewards for themselves, their family members and their cause. In order for the terrorist act to succeed, the suicide terrorist must perish as a result of the attack. Therefore, the suicide terrorist believes this heightens their status in society. "Self-sacrifice is a way of legitimizing a cause, inspiring imitation, and promising individual glory" ("Council on Foreign Relations," 2004, para.3). This quote is crucial to describing the mental state of the suicide terrorist. Suicide bombers are deeply committed to their causes and themselves; "a person who is killed while defending Islam becomes a martyr and is guaranteed a place in paradise with all the attendant benefits, including the services of a number of virgins" (Galak, 2005, p.7). Osama Bin Laden states this belief of martyrdom in his *fatwa*, which is the declaration of war against the United States that he authored in 1996. The Al Qaida told United States' officials: "These youth love death as you love life" (Eggen & Wilson, 2005, p. 2).

Other Models

In addition to the terrorist models outlined above, there are smaller models that fall under the scope of terrorism. For example, cyber-terrorists specialize in manipulating computer systems from afar and as a result, create chaotic problems in society. A cyber-terrorist can utilize his or her computer skills to interfere with emergency communications, disrupt the availability of utilities and disable individual computers, computer networks and the information they contain (Stoessinger, 2005).

Another less-known type of terrorist is the *Eco-terrorist*. This terrorist targets property, not people, for his or her attacks. The Eco-terrorist originally began as a lawful protestor, but evolved into using acts of aggression that result in property damage to the targets of their protests, such as research laboratories and abortion clinics ("Inside the FBI: Eco-Terrorism," 2002).

Additional types of terrorists include disgruntled employees as well as right and left wing activists.

Demographics

Terrorists do not fit into a specific demographic mold. Although particular attention is paid to terrorists of Middle Eastern descent, a terrorist is not any particular race, creed or religious background. In an effort to eliminate such racial profiling, the reader is encouraged to consider the following statistics: Seventy-five to eighty percent of terrorists are single males. Eighteen percent of terrorists proclaim strong religious beliefs. Sixty-six percent of terrorists are of a middle or upper class economic background and sixty-five percent have some college or graduate work (Beiner, 2004).

In some cases, terrorists do come from less fortunate backgrounds, but as these statistics document, the higher percentage of terrorists come from more affluent backgrounds. The combination of a poor economic background and lack of advanced education is apparent in the specialty field of suicide terrorists. Most suicide terrorists are males. However, 15% are female—a figure that is increasing (Beiner, 2004). For further demographical information about terrorists, the reader is referred to the RAND Terrorism Chronology Database that can be located at http://www.rand.org.

Theories of Terrorism

Terrorism experts, psychologists and scholars alike study terrorism. Each discipline offers a different perspective. The lack of terrorists available for direct study contributes to researcher challenges. However, five fundamental sociological theories of terrorism currently exist. They are outlined below:

The Relative Deprivation Hypothesis

Beiner (2004), professor and author of *The Criminology of Terrorism: Theories and Models,* suggests:

> The idea that a person goes about choosing their values and interests, they compare what they have and don't have, as well as what they want or don't

want, with real or imaginary others. The person usually perceived a discrepancy between what is possible for them and what is possible for others, and reacts to it with anger or inflamed sense of injustice. (p. 5)

Criminologists debate whether this theory relates to economic deprivation, or the influence of subjective experiences related to distress and scarcity of those things tangible (Beiner, 2004).

The Moral Disengagement Hypothesis

The Moral Disengagement Hypothesis deals with the ways a terrorist rationalizes actions.

The idea that encompasses all the ways a person neutralizes or removes any inhibitors they have about committing acts of horrific violence. Some common patterns include imagining one's self as a hero, portraying one's self as a functionary, minimizing the harm done, dehumanizing the victim, or insulating one's self in routine activities. (Beiner, 2004, p. 5)

Jerald M. Post, a professor of political psychology and international affairs at George Washington University further hypothesizes that by joining a terrorist group, individuals are able to enhance their sense of belonging and the narcissistic tendencies they previously lacked. Fulfilling the theory of moral disengagements allows the terrorist to justify actions (Hudson, 1999).

The Frustration-Aggression Hypothesis

Beiner (2004) explains "the idea that every frustration leads to some form of aggression, and that every aggressive act relieves that frustration to some extent" (p. 5). This hypothesis is also based on criminology. Those who start off on the wrong side of society end up on a slippery slope, thus layering oneself with a blistering anger which can only lead to a massive explosion at the end.

The Narcissistic Rage Hypothesis

The Narcissistic Rage Hypothesis is the *"What else can go wrong?"* theory. The individual becomes a shadow of gloom perpetuating uncertainty and displeasure at the beginning of one's life. This theory is:

An umbrella idea for all the numerous things that can go wrong in child-rearing, such as too much smothering, too little smothering, ineffective discipline, overly stringent discipline, psychological trauma, coming from a broken home, etc.... that leads to the same effect of a "What about Me?" reaction to a child. (Beiner, 2004, p. 5)

The Negative Identity Hypothesis

The Negative Identity Hypothesis identifies those who want to be someone else and due to pressuring reasons are destined to be unrealistic about who they really are. It is "the idea that, for whatever reason, a person develops a vindictive and covert rejection of the roles and statuses laid out for them by their family, community, or society" (Beiner, 2004, p. 5). This theory addresses the terrorists who deliberately run from what is expected from them in society.

The Group Psychology of Terrorism

Group terrorists are true believers. There is no compromise within the group structure. In their minds, they are forever unaccepted in an ordinary society. "Terrorists tend to submerge their own identities into the group, resulting in a kind *of group mind* and group moral code that requires unquestioned obedience to the group" (Hudson, 1999, p. 39). Group terrorists redefine a goal after that goal is met, and in fearing loss, this triggers a defense mechanism with the group culture. Terrorists within a group setting are unapproachable, for there is power within their group dynamic (Moghaddam & Marsella, 2004). A common part of the terrorist group is that faction known as the *terrorist cell*. A terrorist cell is a way that the group can infiltrate a location undetected to orchestrate and complete an attack ("Terrorism," 2005). The group terrorist will sacrifice his or her own life for that of the group. He or she embraces the philosophical concept of the greater good.

Personality Types

Psychologists describe six different personality types of insurgents most likely to commit terrorist acts of such magnitude that they would result in world mass-destruction (Hudson, 1999). These types include: "paranoids, paranoid schizo-phrenics, borderline mental defectives, schizophrenic types, passive-aggressive personality types, and sociopath personalities" (Hudson, 1999, p. 12). An individual diagnosed with one of the above personality disorders is diagnosed as a *psychotic personality*.

Conclusion

The discipline of psychology contributes to our understanding of actions that motivate terrorists' behaviors. Although psychologists are not able to offer a universal model of a terrorist, they provide insight into the minds—the behaviors—of terrorists. As research continues, a greater understanding will emerge. Through understanding the mind and behaviors of a terrorist, we will be able to take a more proactive approach to effectively protecting ourselves from the horrendous destruction that results from their actions.

The State of Florida:
A Model of Homeland Security

"Florida's response to the September 11th terrorist attacks has been a model of how homeland security coverage should operate at the state level. You've established a security network that is a model for our states and communities all across the country."

—*Vice President Dick Cheney*

Introduction

The attacks of 9/11 brought homeland security issues to the forefront of concerns for all United States citizens. These issues are directly approached at all levels of government. Although many of the implementations set forth nationally are carried over into state and local governments, there are also several things that were implemented by the State of Florida alone, and other modifications that were made by the Southwest Florida region specifically.

Florida's Comprehensive Response Plan

Following the 9/11 World Trade Center attacks, the State of Florida was the first state to have a comprehensive plan for response to terrorist attacks on the desk of President George Bush (Tom Ridge, former Director of Homeland Security, personal interview, July 14, 2005; Dudley Goodlette, Florida State Representative, District 76, personal interview, June 16, 2005). This comprehensive plan was first issued in October 2001 by the Florida Department of Law Enforcement (FDLE) and the State Division of Emergency Management. Florida Governor Jeb Bush officially implemented the plan on October 11, 2001 by Executive Order Number 01-300. The plan became a prototype for other states in the

United States. This order required several things in order to ensure the safety of Florida's residents:

> FDLE will organize a Regional Security Task Force in each of the FDLE'S seven operational regions with dedicated FDLE employees, representatives from Division of Emergency Management, an available representative from the Department of Health, and any appropriate and available county and local official. The goal of each Task Force shall include (i) coordinating domestic security efforts among local, state, and federal resources to ensure such efforts are not fragmented or unnecessarily duplicative; (ii) coordinating appropriate domestic security training for local and state personnel; (iii) coordinating the collection and dissemination of investigative and intelligence information; and (iv) facilitating responses to terrorist incidents within each region. The Task Forces may incorporate other objectives reasonably related to these domestic security goals to account for the variety of conditions and resources present in each region. (Goodlette, 2004, p. 2)

Regional Domestic Security Task Forces

The task forces established by the State of Florida are organized into the sub-categories of Education/Schools, Fire, Rescue, Health/Medical, Communication, Law Enforcement and Emergency Management (Goodlette, 2004). Each task force is assigned specific duties and responsibilities that ensure public safety and improve avenues of communication between the regions. In addition to the development of the Regional Domestic Security Task Forces, the State of Florida established a Domestic Security Oversight Board to administer the duties, ensure consistency, provide communication and demand accountability from the task forces (Goodlette, 2004).

Don Hunter, Collier County Sheriff

Along with the large scale implementations made at state level, local officials in Southwest Florida also made several changes that ensure the safety of citizens in the region. We are very fortunate in Southwest Florida to have our own Collier County Sheriff as the head of the task force for this region. Sheriff Don Hunter is instrumental in implementing many additional safeguards at the local level. One noteworthy improvement to be spawned by the statewide comprehensive plan and utilized to great propensity locally, is the more direct and frequent communication between local and state security officials. Prior to the 9/11 attacks, communication was infrequent. Now, as a result of the comprehensive plan, Sheriff

Hunter has a very close working relationship with the chief of FDLE'S Office of Statewide Intelligence (Sheriff Don Hunter, personal communication, July 8, 2005).

Within our region, Sheriff Hunter created subcommittees with agency heads at the lead to specifically focus on terrorism. There are three people whose only responsibility is to follow domestic security intelligence. Sheriff Hunter stated that their purpose is to, "Develop sources on the street for information before a situation occurs" (Sheriff Don Hunter, personal communication, July 8, 2005). These individuals in turn act as liaisons for both gang violence and domestic security information at each of the six Collier County police sub-stations. "The subcommittees meet monthly for briefings and training" (Sheriff Hunter, personal communication, July 8, 2005).

Collier County: An International Travel Destination

Although we made considerable progress at a local level to ensure the safety of our citizens, these changes will prove effective only if we can encourage uniformity in surrounding counties. In Collier County, we are openly recognized as an international travel destination. This in itself puts us at a greater risk than many other parts of the country. The challenge now is to get other counties around us to understand and begin to tackle some of the issues surrounding these threats. Uniformity is constantly encouraged, but there is still some reluctance to recognize the actual threats that lie within our region. Due to our appeal as an international travel destination, the likelihood of sleeper cells in our area is elevated. In order to provide the highest level of success against the possible dangers, these concerns must be addressed by all the surrounding counties (Sheriff Hunter, personal interview, July 8, 2005).

Conclusion

Florida is looked to as a role model for other states to follow in terms of terrorism preparedness. With our proactive approach, we can minimize the threat to our local region, our state, and ultimately, the United States. The steps that we are taking currently are only the beginning for what should prove to be stepping stones for the highest security measures in place by any local community.

Immigration: New Precautions in Southwest Florida

"Keep, ancient lands, your storied pomp!" cries she with silent lips. "Give me your tired, your poor, your huddled masses yearning to breathe free, the wretched refuse of your teeming shore, send these, the homeless, tempest-tost to me, I lift my lamp beside the golden door!"

—*Emma Lazarus*

Introduction

For hundreds of years people worked, sacrificed, and even died attempting to make the journey to the United States of America—the land of liberty. As Americans, we were proud to welcome immigrants. We understood their need for a better life. However, after the events of 9/11, this attitude changed. Average citizens believed that improvements to how immigrants and visitors were screened before entering our country must be made.

Along with entry procedures, Americans became concerned with how to keep contact with immigrants once they were in our country and how to monitor their expired visas. The April 25, 2001 issue of the *Sun-Sentinel*, a Southwest Florida newspaper, reported that of 807 registered voters polled, 81% indicated more restrictions were needed in regulating immigration (FAIR, 2005).

Immigration and Naturalization Service

The first action on a national level was to disband the Immigration and Naturalization Service (INS) and create two new entities. The first, Immigration

Affairs (IA), is charged with handling applications, processing, status and record keeping for immigrants. The second, Immigration and Customs Enforcement (ICE), now handles the control and prosecution of immigration violations and legal matters.

The government also heightened border security, imposed new restrictions on visas and visitors, and implemented stricter control of passengers and their luggage. All this means more scrutiny and questions for those immigrants entering the United States. We are now more interested in immigrants' motives for coming into the country (Wipf, 2002). In a news conference, Homeland Security Secretary Michael Chertoff announced many changes. For example, first time visitors to the United States will be required to give all ten fingerprints as opposed to the current requirement of two ("Department of Homeland Security," n.d. a).

In a personal interview, a Russian immigrant on a work visa recounted the new changes he experienced in obtaining his driver's license: In Florida, a driver's license is valid for four to six years. The exact amount of time of validity depends on one's driving record. Previously, when a driver's license was issued to an immigrant on a visa, it was given the same expiration date as a U.S. citizen's license even if the immigrant's visa expired earlier. With new security measures, the license will expire at the same time as the visa. Additionally, there is now a 30 day hold on the license for immigrants. This procedure allows time for a background check and to ensure all credentials submitted are legitimate (Wipf, 2002).

Immigrants in Southwest Florida

Florida has the third largest immigrant population in the United States. Only California and New York rank higher. In addition, Florida has the fourth largest immigrant share of the total population. Only New York, California and Hawaii rank higher. More than one of every eight of Florida residents is foreign born. About one in every eleven immigrants in the United States resides in Florida (FAIR, 2004).

Table 1 shows the total population of Florida compared to the foreign born population (FAIR, 2004). Table 2 provides similar figures for the four counties in the Southwest Florida region (FAIR, 2004).

Table 1: Extended Immigration Data for Florida

Extended Immigration Data for Florida

Summary Demographic State Data (and Source)

Population (2004 Census Bureau estimate):	**17,397,161**
Population (2000 Census):	**15,982,378**
Foreign-Born Population (2003 CB estimate):	**2,995,400**
Foreign-Born Population (2000 Census):	**2,670,828**
Share Foreign-Born (2003):	**17.6%**
Share Foreign-Born (2000):	**16.7%**
Immigrant Stock (2000 CB estimate):	**4,637,000**
Share Immigrant Stock (2000 estimate):	**29.0%**
Naturalized U.S. Citizens (2000 Census):	**1,207,502**
Share Naturalized (2000 estimate):	**45.2%**
Legal Immigrant Admission (INS 1993-2002):	**754,692**
Refugee Admission (2001 HHS):	**16,775**
Illegal Alien Population (2003 INS estimate):	**337,000**
Projected Population—2025 (2001 FAIR):	**27,100,400**

Table 2: Immigration Data by County

BREAKDOWN BY COUNTY

Summary Metro Area and County Data (and Source)	COL-LIER	LEE	CHAR-LOTTE	SARA-SOTA	TOTALS
Population (2003CB est.):	286,634	492,210	153,392	346,793	1,226,029
Population (**2000 Census**):	251,377	440,888	141,627	325,957	1,159,849
Foreign-born Population (**2000 Census**):	46,071	40,362	11,292	30,416	128,141
Share Foreign Born (2000):	18.3%	9.2%	8.0%	9.3%	11%
Immigrant Settlement 1991-98 (**INS**):	4,405	3,996	1,516	3,351	13,268
Population Projection 2025 (**FAIR**):	882,500	875,000	260,600	486,000	2,504,100

If the percentage of foreign-born residents remains consistent and projections are accurate, by the year 2025, approximately 27 million legal immigrants will reside in Florida and 2.5 million legal immigrants will reside in Southwest Florida. The figures for illegal immigrants are estimated as we have no true way of tracking them.

With such a large immigrant population there was concern as to whether ICE would be able to keep up with the immigrants in the state. As a result, Florida is privileged to be the test state for local law enforcement personnel to be ICE trained to handle immigration violations. In 2003, 35 deputy sheriffs from the state received ICE training. This training prepares the deputies to detain immigrants who are in violation of their visas. As a result of this program, ICE will now list visa violators in the National Crime Information Center (NCIC), which permits police officers to detain a violator if he or she is apprehended for a lesser offence (Kobach, 2004).

Collier Counter Sheriff Don Hunter informed us that five of the original ICE agents are stationed in Southwest Florida and five newly trained officers, likewise, will be stationed in Southwest Florida. When asked about immigrant detainments since the creation of the task force, Sheriff Hunter replied,

> Previously there were no detainments, now it is done frequently. One example is "Operation Tarmac." Senior ICE agents in the task-force reviewed 5,000 dossiers concerning individuals who raised airport security issues. Of these, there were 52 individuals that had used fraudulent means to become last stage baggage handlers and other sensitive positions. Many of these people were detained, indicted and deported. (Sheriff Don Hunter, personal communication, June 16, 2005)

Racial Profiling

The implementation of this new program raised many questions and concerns about giving such authority to local deputies. In a December 14, 2001 *Sarasota Herald* article, reporter Kevin Valine addressed the trepidations of Southwest Florida Muslims. The Muslims requested the right to have a Muslim present when FDLE officers questioned another Muslim who may have information about terrorism. Attorney General Ashcroft requested about 500 statewide interviews of men in their 20s and 30s who were in Florida on temporary visas from Middle Eastern countries noted for terrorist activities. The concern was that it would cross-over into "racial profiling." Ahmed Elfarai, the Islamic Community spokesman, felt that it would put the interviewees at ease if they had representation—especially if this representation was from countries where the police were feared. The response of the FDLE was that all the interviews were voluntary (Valine, 2001). Sheriff Hunter gave the following response to a question about fears of racial profiling from the Hispanic and Haitian communities.

> Our responsibilities have nothing to do with nationality; we worry about national security. We will go after anyone who is a threat. We will not be persuaded to ignore our responsibilities. We work closely with the Hispanic community to let them know that we are not concerned with doing massive random sweeps; we don't have the desire or the manpower to do so. (Sheriff Don Hunter, personal communication, June 16, 2005).

Conclusion

Anytime there is change, there are growing pains. The new regulations require more scrutiny of immigrants and some innocent people may be inconvenienced. There is weekly news of another arrest or questions being asked of people suspected of threatening our national and local safety. However, considering recent history, it is only natural for our government to err on the side of caution. The new national and Southwest Florida precautions contribute to the security of our citizens. In the proactive efforts to keep our nation secure, individuals' rights may be stressed, but in these trying times we must be cautious and alert.

Water Systems in Southwest Florida: Intensified Security

"Water is life's mater and matrix, mother and medium. There is no life without water.."

—Albert Szent-Gyorgyi

Introduction

One of the most valuable resources in Southwest Florida is the drinking water. Throughout the ages, water sources were viewed as potential targets for vandalism, poisoning and contamination. Even before the terrorist attacks of 9/11, water utilities took precautions against possible interferences from terrorism, poisoning, vandalism and natural disasters. However, since that world-changing day, security has intensified.

Threats to Water Systems

Although there are risks to water utilities, most officials find terrorist threats to water systems quite small (Copeland & Cody, 2005). It would be difficult to create an undetected effort that would damage a large water system. Enormous amounts of contaminates are required to poison a water system. Thus, because of the volume required, these contaminates are easily detected during the process of water production. The Department of the Army is currently conducting intensified research on the detection and removal of various chemical and biological agents from water systems.

As early as 1941, J. Edgar Hoover recognized water utilities as potential targets for terrorists (Copeland & Cody, 2001). Water systems are linked to other infrastructures such as electrical, chemical and transportation. Damage to drinking water production can have far reaching public affects. Disruption to the access of water could also affect first responders' effectiveness in firefighting efforts.

Currently, no federal standards are in place to protect utilities. However, after the 9/11 attacks, vulnerability studies were mandated to protect the nation's various utilities. Monies were budgeted to assess each area's unique needs and make changes to protect these facilities.

Southwest Florida Water Systems

Mel Fisher, Director of Operations at the Bonita Springs Utilities Water and Wastewater Facilities, explains that before 9/11, the largest concern for water utilities was from storm damage and interruption of electricity from hurricanes (Mel Fisher, personal communication, June 17, 2005). Most concerns involve drinking water, but interruption of electricity to a wastewater facility could cause the discharge of untreated water into surface water and ground water systems. This could spread more contamination to the public water system than would a terrorist attack on the facility. With this in mind, utilities are now supplied with emergency generators—an improvement that eliminated interruption of service due to the 2004 Hurricane Charley power outages. Bonita Springs Utilities never lost service to its customers during or after the hurricane, and was able to help provide water to Lee County Utilities through a water distribution system interconnection ("Bonita Springs Utilities," 2004).

Most water and wastewater facilities in Southwest Florida are now fenced in. Fisher pointed out that the Bonita Springs water plant has implemented guards at the gate 24/7/365 (Mel Fisher, personal communication, June 17, 2005). Before the 9/11 event, the gate was not manned, but had a security code for entry to the plant. Now a guard checks all vehicles entering the plant. Outside venders may only enter by appointment, and their drivers are on a pre-approved list. If a driver is not on the list, he is turned away. Inside the plant, computerized identification cards regulate access to various areas. Outside contractors and engineering firms also must comply with employee background checks and are restricted from areas of the plant that do not apply to their contracts.

The situation of outside contractors within public utilities can be a problem. Recently, in a weapons-grade nuclear plant in Tennessee there was a breach of security (Mansfield, 2005). It was reported that several employees of a construction sub-contractor had falsified identification and work permits. The alarming thing is that there were *For Official Use Only* documents in a construction trailer that was open to these undocumented workers. As a result of this incident, contractors will no longer be able to self-certify their staff. All contractors will have to provide documentation regarding workers' identification papers and background checks.

Within the Bonita Springs Water plant, video cameras monitor movements and alarm systems alert the operations team of any unauthorized access. This area of Southwest Florida does not rely on reservoirs. The drinking water is pumped from wells in various parts of the county. These wells are caged, locked and monitored by alarms and cameras. At any time, operators can check on the wells via the computerized operations center.

Mel Fisher was asked how the water plant operators can detect contamination. He described how most contaminates would deplete the chlorine residual, effect the pH, manifest as turbidity, or affect the dissolved oxygen of the water being treated. This would set up alarms, and the water would be tested for contamination (Mel Fisher, personal communication, June 17, 2005).

Hebert (2001) explains that the finished water in the water distribution systems is where the greatest risk lies, and Fisher agrees (Mel Fisher, personal communication, June 17, 2005). All of the access points of water entry to communities are locked and backflow preventers are in the process of being installed. Should a loss of pressure take place due to accidental or deliberate damage, these backflow preventers will prevent the backflow of contaminated water into the system.

Conclusion

Bonita Springs Utilities sets a standard for other water utilities in Southwest Florida. Smaller water and wastewater plants are in the process of implementing similar policies—policies that will ensure that quality drinking and reclaimed water are available and safe for residents. Similar measures are being used in chemical and electrical facilities in the Southwest Florida area. Citizens of Southwest Florida can feel confident that through proactive measures, their water sources are being protected from both natural disasters and terrorist acts.

Southwest Florida First Responders: A Strategy Second to None

"Some will remember an image of a fire or story of a rescue. Some will carry memories of a face and a voice gone forever. And I will carry this. It is the police shield of a man named George Howard who died at the World Trade Center trying to save others. It was given to me by his mom, Arlene, as a proud memorial to her son. It is my reminder of lives that ended and a task that does not end."

—George Bush

Introduction

First responders: America's law enforcement officers, fire fighters, and para-medics provide private citizens with ultimate protection from acts of terrorism. These men and women prove day-in-and-day-out that they are true heroes. When everyone else is running away, these brave people defy human instinct and rush toward fires, gunshots, and screams. Because they are first on the scene, they offer us our greatest hope of lessening the consequences planned by terrorists.

Since first responders make the initial decisions when dealing with a crisis, it is our responsibility to see that they have the proper equipment and training to save lives. It is our first responders who are going to make all the initial decisions when dealing with a crisis. The Department of Homeland Security is committed to ensuring first responders nationwide are "prepared, equipped and trained for any situation…by bringing together information and resources to prepare for and respond to a terrorist attack, natural disaster or other large-scale emergency" ("Department of Homeland Security," n.d. d, para. 2).

The United States has over one million firefighters of which 750,000 are volunteers, 436,000 sworn law enforcement officers, 186,000 sworn sheriff deputies and over 155,000 nationally registered emergency medical technicians ("Orange County Sheriff's Office," 2005). First responders have the extraordinary responsibility of deciphering whether or not they are faced with an actual terrorist attack. They must then determine the most effective and safest way to deal with the situation. They answer the hard questions of how to limit the loss of life, reduce injuries; minimize property damage and finally, how to bring the terrorist to justice. Each first responder plays a crucial role in coordinating this interdisciplinary, interagency operation (Tom Ridge, former director of Homeland Security, personal interview, June 16, 2005).

Law Enforcement

Florida currently employs about 40,000 law enforcement officers ("Florida Department of Law Enforcement," 2001). Major David Palanzi of the Lee County Sheriff's Office is quoted in the *Ft. Myers News-Press* as saying, "Law enforcement must take a different approach than it did before September, 11th" (Boxleitner, 2005, p. B3). Deputies now receive daily threat level information. This information appears on the screen of the computers that they use in the field. Deputies treat all threats as credible.

After 9/11, deputies were charged with the added responsibility of patrolling critical sites. These critical sites include the water, telephone and electric companies, government buildings, radio transmitters, sewage treatment plants, overpasses, hotels, churches and synagogues. Several conditions contribute to the uniqueness of Southwest Florida: 1) The population nearly doubles during the months of February, March and April. 2) Southwest Florida is the home of two Ritz Carlton hotels that attract influential guests. 3) Numerous high-ranking retired military personnel and company executives make their home in the lush tropical surroundings. Each of these conditions requires extra patrols that local law enforcement officers are capable of providing (Collier County Sheriff Don Hunter, personal communication, July 8, 2005).

Statewide Mutual Aid Agreement

One of the few benefits Southwest Florida garnered from the past hurricane seasons is the Statewide Mutual Aid Agreement. In essence, a county affected by a disaster, be it natural or manmade, can ask another county to deploy its resources. These resources include: personnel, equipment, services and supplies. This is all coordinated through the Emergency Management Department ("Collier County Comprehensive Emergency Management Plan," 2005). The deputies have the ability to enforce laws from anywhere within the state.

This interagency cooperation is thought by some to be one of their finest accomplishments. When dealing with a disaster, Collier County Sheriff Don Hunter says they go on 'Alpha Bravo' shift patterns, meaning 12-hour shifts so the presence of law enforcement officers is more visible during that time of turmoil (Collier County Sheriff, Don Hunter, personal communication, July 8, 2005). All deputies are on duty, and all leaves of absences are cancelled. The deputies have a 24-hour response time responsibility to all counties statewide.

Regional Domestic Security Task Force

The Southwest Florida Regional Domestic Security Task Force is led by Collier County Sheriff Don Hunter. Sheriff Hunter takes a proactive stance against terrorism. He is concerned that there is still some reluctance in neighboring counties to recognize the actual threats that lie within our region. Sheriff Hunter points out that because Southwest Florida is an internationally recognized destination, sleeper cells (terrorists working undetected) may be more prevalent than most people realize (Collier County Sheriff, Don Hunter, personal communication, July 8, 2005).

Tabletop Exercises

To ensure that Florida accomplishes its initiative of a unified command, response, and recovery to an act of terrorism, the seven regions participate in tabletop exercises. These are mock, full-scale drills on federal, state and local levels. These exercises give all agencies involved an actual opportunity to use all aspects of their response plans (activation, implementation and execution) to a terrorist event. "Within the structure of these task forces are the unifying disciplines, whether it be law enforcement, fire, EMS, emergency management health, hospitals or education, that come together to develop plans, procedures and protocols to prepare for, respond to, and recover from, any act of terrorism." (Dipietre, 2005, para. 4).

These exercises may take the form of a round-table discussion or a field exercise. Exercises such as these determine what works and what doesn't during a crisis situation. Each year we work to enhance our domestic security strategy and implement new measures designed to protect our state. Each year domestic security strategy is enhanced and new measures are implemented to protect our state. "Our citizens and visitors can be proud of the fact that Florida has put together a sound strategy that is second to none" (Dipietre, 2005, para. 9).

At the third annual mock terrorism tabletop exercise held in Tallahassee, Governor Jeb Bush said "Florida is better prepared today to fight terrorism, thanks to the phenomenal team work developed during the past hurricane season. Our strength comes from the ongoing commitment to train and learn better ways to protect our residents and visitors against terrorist activity and the impacts of natural disasters" ("Dogged Determination," 2005, para. 2). According to the Leaders Outline 2005-06 Domestic Security Priorities for Florida, since 9/11, the state has allotted more than $740 million in federal and state funds to domestic security. By the end of 2005, all of Florida's regional task forces will have completed tabletop and field exercises (Dipietre, 2005).

The tabletop training was put to use on September 12, 2002. A couple at a Shoney's restaurant in Georgia overheard three men of Middle Eastern descent discussing the fact that although others mourned the events of 9/11, these men celebrated. The conversation continued with the men claiming that on September 13th, Americans would mourn again. They said they were going to Miami and were behind schedule. One man then remarked, "We do not have enough to bring it down" (Husty, 2002, p 1A). The couple jotted down the makes and models of cars and license tags, and a detailed description of the three men and alerted authorities. This diligence aided Collier County deputies in stopping both cars as they attempted to pass through the toll plaza on Alligator Alley. The assisting officer had a bomb sniffing dog who "alerted on both vehicles, which means he identified something that smelled like explosives" (Husty, 2002, p. 1A).

A full excerpt from the story reveals:

> A robot from the Miami-Dade bomb squad searched the cars, took pictures and retrieved some belongings from the cars. The robot could not get to some other items. Bomb technicians, wearing 100-pound protective blast suits, lumbered up to the cars in the sweltering afternoon heat. They worked in shifts of two for 20 minutes each because that's all they could stand, said Sgt. Pete Andreu, Miami-Dade police spokesman. They used ropes for hooks to snag the luggage and pull it free of the cars. An FBI device that detects radioactivity was flown to the scene by a Broward County sheriff's helicopter. All the belongings were X-rayed and screened. The results were negative for any kind of explosives or other weapons of mass destruction. Technicians went over the car again with swabs and again found nothing. Deputies searched the

interstate shoulders on both sides from the tollgate to where the cars were stopped. They found nothing, Hunter said. (Husty, 2002 p. 1A, 11A)

Although it was an expensive operation, it was important for these officials to see theory become reality. "Hunter said the exercise shows the anti-terrorism task force concept works, even if the threat wasn't real" (Husty, 2002, p. 11A). Jerry Sanford, spokesman for the North Naples Fire Department, stated, "This is what a task force is for. Everybody did their job well…Everything was handled well. Everybody was coordinated. Each agency was doing its job. Nobody was stepping on anybody's toes" (Ruane, 2002, p. 11A).

Pete Andreu, spokesman for the Miami-Dade Police Department said "Law enforcement deserves a pat on the back. It's great police work, excellent police work. The interception of the men by the deputy at the toll gate was phenomenal" (Ruane, 2002, p. 11A). Up to 100 people responded from 19 federal, state and local law enforcement and emergency agencies (Husty, 2002). Lee County Public Safety Director John Wilson said, "Working with the agencies and task force helped to make what happened today a reality. It's testimony to how serious law enforcement folks are taking this and are willing to share information" (Ruane, 2002, p. 10A).

When asked about their performance Hunter said,

> So far the task force passed the test because of Stone's credible report giving details of what she heard the men say, the cars they were driving and the tag number of one of the cars. His deputies stopped the cars. His police dog detected explosives in the cars. Supporting agencies—bomb squads, hazardous materials teams, federal agents, paramedics and firefighters and several others-all worked together. At the time, the nation was under the second highest level of security alert. We believed we were going to receive another attack. So, at the moment if I had to do it over again, I'd do it the same way. (Husty, 2002, p. 14A)

Bomb Squad

One of the benefits garnered from the Department of Homeland Security is the amount of federal grant money allocated to the states. At the time of the Alligator Alley incident, the closest available bomb squad was in Miami. Sheriff Hunter, utilizing federal grant money, established a local bomb squad. The squad acquired bomb suits, a bomb disposal trailer, 2 portable x-ray machines and a water blast shot gun that can be used to render a bomb useless.

Technicians attend a five-week school. Currently, Collier County has three certified technicians. Three more will be trained. They are on call to all counties within the southwest regional task force area. Collier County Sheriff Don Hunter claims that Web sites teaching anyone how to make a bomb take the concept of freedom of speech too far (personal communication, July 8, 2005). An internet Google search for *how to make a bomb* listed 11,200,000 sites. Searching *bomb making instructions* revealed 602,000 sites. With so much information available to the ill-intentioned, Southwest Florida citizens are comforted with the knowledge that Sheriff Don Hunter takes a proactive and interdisciplinary approach to protecting citizens from terrorist attacks.

Special Weapons and Tactics (SWAT) Team

Sheriff Hunter's biography, on the Collier County Sheriff's Office Web site, reports that he developed and now commands the Collier County Sheriff's Special Weapons and Tactics Team (SWAT Team) ("Collier County Sheriff's Office," n.d.). Sheriff Hunter personally appointed all 40 members of the team, ten of which serve full-time.

One of the major law enforcement policy changes was not in response to 9/11, but to the shootings at Columbine. Law enforcement policy, universally, had been to treat situations like Columbine as a hostage situation. The area would be secured and negotiations would begin while waiting for a SWAT team to arrive. This policy needed to change because the motivations of the terrorists had changed. Terrorists today are concerned with body counts and headlines. Now, once four officers arrive on the scene they engage an active shooter and terminate him before he can cause mass casualties. In addition, deputies are better equipped with more accurate, long-distance rifles that hold more ammunition.

Full-time Collier County deputy Corporal Bob Brown says Collier County's SWAT team members believe strongly in a preemptive strike. They have a firm conviction that good intelligence works hand-in-hand with good tactile training. They spend at least 21 hours a month participating in organized training. The ten full-time deputies act as cadre and instruct not only the SWAT team members but other members of law enforcement. It can take up to 30 to 45 minutes for the SWAT team to arrive on scene and don their 60 pounds of gear. Rapid response limits the loss of life. Thus, the establishment of the Quad concept known as *the first four officers at a scene* was developed. This concept incorporates multiple jurisdictions and disciplines. These officers can be deputies, city police, Florida highway patrol, fish and game or alcohol tobacco and firearms officers, all having been trained in this first protocol (Corporal Bob Brown, personal communication, July 22, 2005).

With the Sheriff Hunter's sanction, Corporal Bob Brown and other law enforcement officers in Collier County created a tactical training corporation entitled *Redline-Blueline, Inc.* This organization provides training in counter-terrorism protocols, defense tactics, active-shooter strategies and rapid-response procedures. This training is conducted for law enforcement officers and military personnel. Redline-Blueline also holds civilian classes in self-defense and shooting. In addition, Redline-Blueline teaches members of corporations, churches, and synagogues how to interface effectively with law enforcement personnel. This heightened awareness lessens vulnerability to terrorist attacks (Corporal Bob Brown, personal communication, July 22, 2005).

Emergency Medical Technicians and Paramedics

An Emergency Medical Technician (EMT) attends school for four months, and then must pass a state exam. A paramedic is an EMT who continues his or her education for another 18 months and must pass a national registry exam. In 2000, Collier County Emergency Medical Squadron—the organization that employs EMTs—was named *Provider of the County.* In 2002, it was named *Florida Provider of the Year.* Street care in Collier County is second to none. The newest trend being implemented is cross-training firefighters and paramedics. These interdisciplinary professionals are better able to serve their community.

Contained Escort Teams

Yet another organization prepared to protect the citizens of Southwest Florida is the contained escort team (CET). CET members are EMTs, paramedics and SWAT team members. Each plays an integral role in CET. Once the threat is contained and partially secured, the SWAT team performs a synergistic rescue. The SWAT team acts as a protective escort for the EMTs and paramedics. Whether threatened from an active shooter of an improvised explosive device (I.E.D.), the team forms a 360 degree security envelope around the EMTs and paramedics. Evacuation is the highest priority. The role of the paramedic in the CET is to make quick assessments and grab those who can be stabilized. All the equipment must be carried on backs of team members. Because they are less bulky and easier to carry, tarps are used to carry out the injured instead of backboards and stretchers. Often the SWAT team will set up a safe-room inside the site, which is used as a triage or field hospital. Meanwhile, outside, there is an EMT liaison responsible for placing ambulances and medical helicopters, checking equipment, gathering teams, and replenishing backpacks. Other EMTs will care for the injured who are brought out. For this system to work effectively, EMTs, paramedics and SWAT team members must have total confidence in each other. They must act as one team (Corporal Bob Brown, personal communication, July 22, 2005).

The size of the CET is determined by the number of victims. Corporal Bob Brown says Collier County has developed CET training above and beyond anything that is currently available anywhere else in the country (Personal communication, 2005). We must remember that the EMTs and paramedics never signed up to enter an active shooting scene. This is strictly voluntary, and again demonstrates that they are true heroes.

Firefighters

Fire departments train to respond to natural disasters such as hurricanes, tornadoes, floods and earthquakes as well as both accidental and premeditated man-made disasters. This makes them the quintessential all-hazard response team. On 9/11 at the World Trade Center, their selflessness cost New York City 343 of its finest citizens. Since the mid-1900s, training to be alert for threats of weapons of mass destruction and other terrorist activities has been on the minds of firefighters. They are trained to look for secondary bombs after an initial explosion. Firefighters stay away from unknown biological and chemical toxins without the proper equipment and protection. They have also been trained in the preserving of evidence and how best to coordinate with other agencies ("Counsel on Foreign Relations," n.d.).

Because they are often first on the scene, local fire departments are often the first line of protection in any occurrence. Firefighters not only put out fires but are also responsible for providing emergency medical services and working with hazardous materials. Locally, firefighters received advanced hazardous material and weapons of mass destruction training. They are knowledgeable about trucks containing liquid oxygen, propane and chlorine. A substantial amount of federal grant money is spent on hazardous materials training. Firefighters consider a one mile radius around a hazardous material scene the hot zone. In addition, firefighters are trained to look for other extenuating factors such as dead wild life and weather clouds (Southwest Florida fire fighter, personal communication, July 25, 2005).

Along with EMS, firefighters are also part of the Disaster Response Team. They are also trained in urban search and rescue, both technical and large scale like the Value Jet incident. Fire districts do not always duplicate all of their services. Like law enforcement, the fire districts participate in mutual aid to support or cover districts while they are fighting fires. Upon request the district will send 'strike teams' to other counties. All involved agencies operate from the incident command system. This system keeps track of all the participants at the scene. The highest ranking officer runs the scene, or they defer to experience.

Conclusion

When thinking of all the disciplines that first responders practice daily, the list seems endless. They must play the role of a psychologist, mentor, technician, chemist, police officer, trainer, lawyer (both legal and case law), doctor, nurse, surgeon, politician, mediator, weatherman, scientist, psychic, communication specialist, researcher, and sociologist who looks at culture as well as diversity. These men and women who have chosen a career in one of the disciplines that fall under first responder are extraordinary people. They have not become complacent since 9/11. They are, indeed, true heroes and heroines.

Preparedness:
Each Citizen's Responsibility

"Much like homeland security in general, America's preparedness requires everyone's help. That's why we've called you together—to continue building an important partnership—one that will result in an enduring and successful strategy for emergency preparedness across the country."

—*Secretary of Homeland Security, Tom Ridge*

Introduction

In Southwest Florida we prepare for hurricanes, but are we prepared for an act of terrorism? Average civilians are usually the first on the scene after a disaster. Do we know what to do in those few minutes before the first responders arrive? The Department of Homeland Security (DHS) advises us that being prepared for a terrorist attack is the responsibility of every American ("Department of Homeland Security," n.d.).

From a DHS fact sheet on citizen preparedness, we learn:

> At the Department of Homeland Security, we are hard at work creating and implementing preparedness plans; developing procedures and policies that will guide our actions in the event of a terrorist attack; conducting training and exercises to ensure that our first responders possess a necessary level of preparedness; enhancing partnerships with state and local governments, private sector institutions and other organizations; and funding the purchase of much-needed equipment for first responders, states, cities, and towns. These activities, along with an active American community, contribute to a level of national preparedness that is critical to achieving our goal of a better prepared America. ("Department of Homeland Security," n.d. b, para. 1)

Ready Campaign

Homeland security does not focus solely on national security. In 2003, DHS ran a national advertising campaign called the *Ready Campaign* ("Ready.Gov U.S. Department of Homeland Security," n.d). It was a public service campaign intended to educate and empower United States' citizens who may be required to respond to terrorist attacks and other disasters. More information about this campaign can be found at www.dhs.gov.

Citizen Corps

Also under DHS is the Citizen Corps. Their mission is "to harness the power of every individual through education, training and volunteer service to make communities safer, stronger, and better prepared to respond to the threats of terrorism, crime, public health issues and disasters of all kinds" ("Citizen Corps," n.d., para. 1). This is accomplished through a national network of state, local and tribal Citizen Corps Councils. Citizen Corps trains individuals to have a disaster plan and a kit with supplies. They offer classes in emergency preparedness, response capabilities, first aid, CPR, fire suppression and search and rescue procedures. And finally, they get individuals involved with volunteers.

In the event of a terrorist attack, volunteers support first responders and disaster relief groups. In 95% of all emergencies, bystanders or victims themselves are the first to provide emergency assistance or to perform a rescue (Citizen Corps, n.d.).

Community Emergency Response Team

The Community Emergency Response Team (CERT) is another Homeland Security disaster preparation program with the goal of encouraging people in the community to become involved with protecting our country from terrorists. CERT is active in Southwest Florida. CERT is comprised of a group of concerned citizens who volunteer to take seven weeks of training that "enhances their ability to recognize, respond to, and recover from a major emergency or disaster" ("Collier County Emergency Management," n.d., para. 3). In-field CERT teams are recon teams. They are key players in reporting the resources our communities need to protect us from terrorist attacks.

A Family Emergency Plan

We have plans at schools and on airplanes. It only makes sense to have a plan at home—the place where we spend the most time. Creating a family emergency plan begins with choosing someone from out of town to be the emergency contact. This person should live far enough away so as not to be affected by your potential emergency. Inform your contact that he or she may receive a call. Make sure each family member knows your contact's phone number. Phone lines may be down or busy so be patient but persistent. Also decide on a designated meeting area. Be sure to give a copy of your emergency plan to your child's school or daycare. Know the school or daycare's emergency plan. It is important for our children to see us being vigilant.

The second step is to assemble a disaster kit. This kit should sustain you for three days. Include non-perishable food, water, a can opener, baby formula and medicine. It should also contain flashlights, batteries, battery-operated radio, candles, matches, a whistle, a first aid kit, toiletries, change of clothes, bedding, money, important documents, disposable plates, cups, silverware and garbage bags. This kit should be packed and ready to go in case of evacuation ("Collier County Comprehensive Emergency Management Plan," 2005).

Conclusion

After the stress of 9/11, it is reassuring to know that with some preparation we as private citizens can exert a measure of control over terrorist attacks. If we ignore the possibility of a terrorist attack, we are not being prudent. Improving our national preparedness is not solely a job for the professionals such as officers of the law and firefighters. All Americans are responsible for learning about potential threats. In the event of a terrorist attack, the average citizen must be prepared to act. Although there is no way to predict what might happen, or what an individual's personal circumstances might be, there are simple things each citizen can do now to prepare his or her home, community and loved ones against the possibility of a terrorist attack.

Hospitals in Southwest Florida: Advanced Level of Preparedness

"I will use treatment to help the sick according to my ability and judgment"

—Hippocrates (460-370 B.C.)

Introduction

As first responders, hospitals are in many ways the backbone of all agencies. At a moment's notice, they must be prepared to handle an incident caused by terrorism. Although this statement could be used to describe any of the first responder agencies, what sets hospitals apart is that they routinely handle crisis situations in their emergency rooms. Hospital emergency rooms, which are generally staffed to meet the every day needs of the community, must also be prepared for the influx of victims from a terrorist incident. In order to meet this demand, many hospitals created terrorism response plans.

Naples Community Hospital

Naples Community Hospital (NCH) in Naples, Florida developed a state-of-the-art plan that is ready to implement at a moment's notice should the area be victimized by terrorists. The plan details what NCH will do to prepare for, implement, and maintain a terrorism incident response protocol that is consistent with the bioterrorism guidelines established by the Centers for Disease Control and Prevention. NCH's plan also meets the criteria established by Collier County Emergency Management as well as the Florida Comprehensive Emergency Plan (Kandace Martin, R.N., NCH, personal communication, June 25, 2005).

After 9/11, Collier County conducted an assessment of its vulnerability to a terrorist attack. The assessment indicated that there are numerous potential targets within the area. This study led to a new awareness of the service needs that NCH and other first response organizations would have to fulfill. Up to that point, the healthcare system was not operating at an optimal level. Training for such incidents was limited and the hospitals were not adequately prepared to deal with the aftermath of a terrorist attack ("Naples Community Hospital," 2001). In response, NCH collaborated with Collier County Emergency Management to develop an incident response plan.

Terrorism Incident Response Plan

The Terrorism Incident Response Plan (TIRP) encompasses the entire NCH Health Care System in both Collier and Lee Counties. It was devised to deal with the four major types of terrorists threats: 1) biological, 2) chemical, 3) radiological and 4) ballistic. The TIRP incorporates contingencies for all facets of emergency response including procedures, supplies, and training. Medical responders are shown the correct treatments for victims and are provided with the correct equipment and protocol to protect them from contamination through TIRP sponsored programs.

Medical responders are also schooled in the proper procedures for handling explosives and incendiary devices. Another component of TIRP is the list of pharmaceuticals that such personnel must be prepared to obtain, store and utilize in the event of an attack. Such measures may appear normal until one considers that the materials in question include vaccines, immune globulin, antibiotics and botulinium anti-toxin medications that are specifically designed to counter the effects of terrorist incidents ("Naples Community Hospital," 2001).

Protection from Bioterrorism

Although TIRP is concerned with all four categories of weapons of mass destruction, its primary focus is on biological threats. Bioterrorism, unlike other forms of attack can be carried out covertly. It also creates a situation that leads rapidly to illness. These facts make it impractical to wait for a formal diagnosis. Instead, NCH developed protocols to handle the high-risk syndromes that are affiliated with each known biological agent ("Naples Community Hospital," 2001).

The entire NCH Health Care System created procedures that will allow for the best treatment possible in the event of a large scale exposure to a biological agent. The clinics, emergency rooms and labs will be the first parts of the hospital to see victims of a bioterrorism outbreak. The NCH policies allow the infection control committee and designated epidemiologist to rapidly implement prevention and control when there is reason to believe a bioterrorist event occurred. The incident command system that uses an interdisciplinary approach to organizing the first response teams is implemented. This plan allows NCH to partner with the Collier County Health Department, the Collier County Sheriff's Department, the Centers for Disease Control and Prevention and Emergency Management. This team may determine that it is necessary to establish an Emergency Operations Center to handle the myriad of details demanded after a bioterrorist attack. Media relations experts from the various agencies work to create a smooth flow of interdepartmental communication and to keep the public informed (Kandace Martin, R.N., NCH, personal communication, July 3, 2005).

Patient Prioritization

Hospitals, which are generally filled to capacity, must be able to prioritize patients during such disasters. Low priority patients can be moved to a different part of the hospital or to another location if necessary. Many such patients are also treated and released to make room for the more seriously afflicted. Local hospitals in Southwest Florida established a network that allows them to work together to facilitate such arrangements. These organizations will work together as a single unit to ensure that the situation is handled with the utmost speed and skill (Kandace Martin, R.N., NCH, personal communication, July 3, 2005).

Conclusion

The proactive approach by NCH and its affiliated district agencies ensures that the safety, security, and competency of emergency healthcare in Collier County continues to meet the requirements established by the Department of Homeland Security. It also establishes Collier County as one of the best-equipped areas in the country to deal with the aftermath of a terrorist attack. This knowledge gives the citizens of Southwest Florida an elevated level of confidence in the local health care system.

Security on the Water

"The superior man, when resting in safety, does not forget that danger may come. When in a state of security he does not forget the possibility of ruin. When all is orderly, he does not forget that disorder may come. Thus his person is not endangered, and his states and all their clans are preserved."

—Confucius

Introduction

The unique qualities of Southwest Florida and how they affect our security have been a recurrent theme throughout this book. Nowhere is this more obvious than the safety of our waterways. The fact that we are a coastal region, while influencing our overall security policies, is not unique. What does make Southwest Florida different from other waterfront areas is both the type of watercraft that is prevalent and the rapidly expanding use of our waterways. While other Florida seaports are hubs of trade and commerce, Southwest Florida is home to a growing number of privately owned pleasure crafts. While this might appear to make security on our waterways a minor issue, the opposite is true because this type of vessel is not subject to the same level of regulatory scrutiny as commercial ships. Therefore, local officials must use other means to counter the possible security threat that this boating population poses. The Coast Guard has answered this challenge through the use of volunteer and citizen organizations, which can function in ways that the government cannot.

America's Waterway Watch

The high volume of boating here in Southwest Florida requires a large Coast Guard presence. In Collier County alone there are four flotillas manned completely by auxiliary volunteers. The main purpose of this organization is public education on the various aspects of water safety, including how to be alert to suspicious activity that could signify a terrorist threat (Lt. Nelson Santiago, U.S. Coast Guard, personal communication, Aug. 23, 2005).

Boaters trained by the Auxiliary Coast Guard form the foundation of America's Waterway Watch (AWW), a public outreach program that increases safety on our waterways by utilizing the boating public. AWW is an interagency effort similar to the Coast Watch program active during World War II. Members are trained to detect and report any questionable activities on the water and along the coast. While AWW is nationwide, every geographic region has adopted it to suit the area's specific needs ("America's Waterway Watch," n.d.).

Operation on Guard

Southwest Florida's incarnation of the initiative is *Operation on Guard*. This program, Operation on Guard, is designed to unite Team Coast Guard—active duty, reserve, and auxiliary, Federal Bureau of Investigation, U.S. Customs Service, U.S. Immigration and Naturalization Service, Florida Department of Law Enforcement, and the American public in response to possible terrorist activity. It creates an effective deterrent measure that employs the eyes and ears of the marine industry and the boating public ("Operation on Guard," n.d.). The Coast Guard believes these are the people who know the coastline best. This is where they live, work and spend their recreation time.

Part of Operation on Guard is the placement of 24" x 36" metal signs that list the reporting criteria with a toll free telephone number for the National Response Center in Washington, D.C. ("Operation on Guard," n.d.). Many Southwest Floridians have seen these signs as they are placed where they will have the most impact. Boaters will notice them where *No Wake Zone, Manatee Zone and Idle Speed Zone* signs are posted. They will also notice them at boat ramps, refueling stations, dock master houses, and municipal docks.

When a call is received by the National Response Center it is determined which agency would be best suited to handle the incident. Then it is forwarded to that agency. If the situation is an emergency it is transferred to the local 911 operator ("Operation on Guard," n.d.). The key is to create the quickest response possible. This will help prevent the situation from increasing in scale and reduce the chance of injury or even death.

Conclusion

Even though Southwest Floridians do not have the same waterway conditions as Miami or Tampa, they do share the same concerns for safety and security. The agencies responsible for water safety in our area have had to be creative in their efforts, incorporating both the boating public and volunteer outreach programs to ensure the safety of our citizens. The strong presence of the United States Coast Guard and their auxiliary programs enable Southwest Floridians to feel that our waterways are a safe and secure environment to work in, spend our recreation time on and live near.

Surface Transportation:
The Future for Southwest Florida

*"Never give in. Never, never, never, never, in nothing great or small,
large or petty, never give in except to convictions of honour and good
sense. Never yield to force; never yield to the apparently overwhelm-
ing might of the enemy."*

—*Sir Winston Churchill*

Introduction

This chapter of the case study addresses the potential vulnerability of Southwest Florida's surface transportation systems. It examines the infrastructure:
roads, bridges and railways. It describes the threat posed to various modes of
transport such as trucks, automobiles and mass transit. Additionally, it analyzes
steps the trucking industry has implemented in order to help prevent the next terrorist attack and whether the techniques employed by that industry can be tailored to fit other industries. Lastly, it offers speculation about the future of
surface transportation in Southwest Florida.

The Terrorist's Favorite Mode of Travel

For many years, particularly during the 1970s, aircraft high-jacking was used
extensively as a form of terrorism. Typically, terrorists would take control of an
aircraft and demand the release of incarcerated terrorists being held by foreign
governments in return for the release of the aircraft and its passengers. As governments implemented security measures making high-jacking an aircraft more difficult, terrorists turned to more common forms of transportation.

The devastating attacks on the World Trade Center resulted in increased security at American airports. This may cause the terrorist to shift back to surface transportation to facilitate their hatred. Historically, trucks, buses, automobiles, and trains were terrorists' favored vehicles used to carry out their evil deeds. A brief look at recent history reveals an interesting pattern that may help us in predicting future attacks.

U.S. Marine Barracks, Beirut, Lebanon

On April 18, 1983, a portion of the United States' Embassy in Beirut, Lebanon collapsed when a van filled with 2000 lbs. of explosives was detonated. Sixty-three people were killed. Hezbollah took credit for that attack. In October of that same year, 241 service members lost their lives when members of Hezbollah drove a truck filled with 20,000 pounds of explosives through several checkpoints and destroyed the United States' Marine Barracks. Minutes later another explosion killed 58 French soldiers nearby (Emery, 2004).

The Oklahoma City Bombing

April 19, 1995, shortly after 9:00 a.m., a large yellow truck parked in front of the Alfred P. Murrah Federal Building in Oklahoma City. Hundreds of government employees began their day with the same routine as any other day. As parents dropped their children off in the building's childcare center, a loud explosion was heard and felt for miles. The result was 168 dead and countless lives destroyed by the actions of two men. Home-grown terrorists Timothy McVeigh and Terry Nichols would later be found guilty of committing, what was at the time, the worst terrorist attack on American soil ("The Bombing," 1996).

Mass Transit Systems and Mass Killings

In 1995, Japanese cult members set off a series of Sarin Gas attacks in the Tokyo subway system in which 12 people perished and over 5,000 were injured. In 1996, Hamas exploded bus bombs in Jerusalem killing 26 innocent people. In June of that same year, a truck explosion targeting United States' troops hit Khobar Towers in Saudi Arabia and left 19 dead. In 1998, the United States' embassies in Nairobi, Kenya and Dar-es-Salaam Tanzania were targets of car bombs resulting in 257 deaths for which Al-Qaeda was blamed. February of 2004, as morning commuters in Madrid, Spain headed for work, explosions tore through 4 trains, killing 191 and injuring 1,200. The list goes on and on with much the same results: death, injury, and destruction. Each incidence has one goal: striking fear and terror into the minds of the population (Emery, 2004). Most recently Left and Oliver (2005) of the London newspaper, *The Guardian*, reported that simultaneous bus and subway bombings left many dead and hundreds wounded.

Identify Threats, Assign Priorities, and Develop Strategies

After the 9/11 attacks on the World Trade Center and the Pentagon, many agencies conducted research on how to better prepare for and prevent a terrorist attack. With a limited amount of resources at the state and local levels, states look to the federal government for funding that would reduce their vulnerability. In 2002, the American Association of State Highway and Transportation Officials (AASHTO) and the Federal Highway Administration (FHWA) convened a blue ribbon panel to identify ways of protecting our infrastructure. Particular interest was placed on bridges and tunnels. The panel developed steps that agencies can take to prioritize and assess risks, thereby utilizing the limited resources where they are most needed ("The Blue Ribbon Panel on Bridge and Tunnel Security," 2003).

The panel identified the following potential threats to transportation: low tech and high tech conventional explosives, truck size or barge size conventional explosives, chemical and biological agents released in tunnels, incendiary devices, hazardous materials in tunnels, and intentional ramming of ships or barges. By recognizing threats, and identifying an area's vulnerabilities, agencies can determine the countermeasures to employ against an attack. Some countermeasures require prioritization and risk assessment and cost benefit analysis.

Taking Steps to Deter an Attack

The panel offers the following explanation on the use of countermeasures: "Countermeasures are often grouped into actions of technologies to deter attack, deny access, detect presence, defend the facility, or design structural hardening to minimize consequences to an acceptable level" ("The Blue Ribbon Panel on Bridge and Tunnel Security," 2003, para. 3).

There are many preventative steps that can be taken to thwart a terrorist attack. This includes increasing the number of visible security personnel, installing cameras and chemical sensors in subways, or removing parking spaces from under or near bridges. These are ways to make the infrastructure less attractive and more complicated for the potential terrorist. In fact, security cameras were instrumental in the identification of the terrorists responsible for the London bombings on July 7, 2005.

Securing the infrastructure is an enormous task. With cooperation from the private sector, state and federal governments are utilizing emerging technologies and tried-and-true techniques to prevent attacks. One positive step taken since 9/11 is the improved interagency cooperation and communication contributing to deterring the next attack. Increased awareness in the government and among private citizens is making it more difficult for the terrorists to strike. Great strides have been made to protect our surface transportation systems. One part of the private sector taking a proactive role in getting their employees involved is the trucking industry.

Breaker One-Nine: Americas Trucking Industry

Millions of tractor-trailer rigs, fuel tankers and large trucks of all kinds traverse our roads on a daily basis. Many of the truckers that operate these massive vehicles in the private sector regularly travel the same roads and are able to pick up on patterns that appear to be out of the norm. On December 17, 2003, President Bush signed Homeland Security Presidential Directive 7. In the directive, President Bush calls for the federal government to coordinate with the private sector to develop an information sharing system facilitating the sharing of information between sectors critical to protecting the nation's key resources ("Homeland Security, Presidential Directive/Hspd-7," 2003).

Within the transportation sector, the American Trucking Association (ATA), working with state trucking associations and other transportation associations, has implemented the Highway Watch (HWW) program. Utilizing grants from the Federal Government, truckers are trained in techniques to assist law enforcement and the intelligence communities in helping to deter terrorist attacks that could cripple our economy.

Anti-Terrorism Action Plan

The HWW program also has an Anti-Terrorism Action Plan (ATAP), which is in keeping with guidance given by the Department of Homeland Security (DHS) ("Highway Information Sharing and Analysis Center," 2005). The goal is to keep this vital portion of our economy from being disrupted. The program also facilitates information sharing, enabling the industry to conduct background checks on its employees. The ATAP has the following goals: establish an industry operations center; develop preparedness and response strategies that work with governmental threat warnings, new technologies, and security and criminal background checks; expand liaison with United States' government agencies along with that of their Mexican and Canadian counterparts.

Interestingly, the USA PATRIOT Act requires that drivers carrying hazardous materials receive a fingerprint-based criminal history and immigration checks. As of January 31, 2004, states are prohibited from issuing a hazardous material endorsement to new applicants until a security threat assessment including fingerprinting is completed by the Transportation Safety Administration (Petri, 2005).

Southwest Florida's Highways and Byways

According to David Price of the FHWA, "America's highway system contains 4 million highway miles, almost 600,000 bridges, and 400 highway related tunnels-with 5 million passenger miles traveled annually and 72% of United States' freight moved across the system in some manner" (Price, 2002, p.1). Southwest Florida has approximately 3,286.2 lane miles of roads and 1,592 bridges ("Florida Department of Transportation," 2004).

The immense size and complexity of the surface transportation system makes it nearly impossible to completely secure it from all terrorist attacks. The cost of safeguarding all surface transportation including mass transit systems, based on the aviation model, would be monumental. Resulting price increases would render surface transportation impractical, inefficient, and time consuming for travelers.

Security in Southwest Florida

What can be done in Southwest Florida to ensure that our surface transportation system is as secure as possible? During a recent interview, Sheriff Don

Hunter stated that in Collier County, certain deputies are assigned to *liaison teams* that conduct daily checks on bridges. They log each visit, and they are keen to detect any changes on or around these bridges and overpasses. When asked about security of the local bus transit system, Sheriff Hunter replied that the onus falls mainly on the bus operators. They are the front-line of defense in spotting certain key signals that a potential terrorist may be targeting their bus. For example, drivers are trained to notice clothing that would be considered out of the norm for Southwest Florida and could conceal a bomb. Sheriff Hunter stated that if the driver is attentive, damage could be minimized (Sheriff Don Hunter, personal communication, July 8, 2005).

Another way to protect our vulnerabilities is to go on the offensive. Within each of the eight sheriff substations, a series of teams that mirror a gang task force set about the community searching for any potential intelligence that may lead to suspicious terrorism related chatter. "Officers are proactive in their approach to getting to know their neighborhoods and being able to prevent an attack by gathering information from the community" (Sheriff Don Hunter, personal communication, July 8, 2005). It was obvious from the interview with Sheriff Hunter that he takes the threat of a terrorist attack seriously and is prepared with a proactive plan that will protect citizens of Southwest Florida.

What Can Each Individual Do?

Individuals can take steps to deter or minimize the outcome of an attack. Firstly, the same as a police officer, each citizen must develop a keen awareness of his or her surroundings. Start with your block or neighborhood. Then expand your ability to detect unusual patterns or objects when traveling to and from work, schools and malls. Each of us must be able to identify atypical behavior and activities, and then take action by contacting someone in authority. This will give the authorities additional intelligence and information they can use.

Training courses, similar to the ones given to the truck operators under the HWW program, are also available to private citizens. If terrorists are not only worried of being suspected by law enforcement, but also by an informed, trained and vigilant public, the resulting deterrent affect makes us all safer.

Local governments continue to focus on enforcement as a major part of their effort in combating terrorism. When interviewed, the director of Facilities Management for Collier County, Skip Camp stated, "What the employee or citizen sees is critical. Most often the general public fails by not reporting what they see that is suspicious around them, sort of how people pass by the scene of an acci-dent and don't call anyone" (personal communication, June 23, 2005).

Israel: A Potential Model

For centuries, Israel has dealt with surface transportation terrorism. Thou-sands of innocent civilians from around the globe have been lost in these attacks. Throughout the years, Israelis have learned approaches to deter and detect attacks before they happen. Perhaps, like Israel, one day Americans will have armed secu-rity forces throughout the mass transportation systems on a permanent basis. Bomb and chemical detection dogs, cameras and sensors may one day be com-monplace.

Conclusion

Will citizens demand that face recognition software systems be added to pub-lic places in order to recognize not only terrorist suspects in the databases but also criminals, or missing children? Will we see an even greater use of x-ray machines to detect explosives, not only for baggage at the airports, but also at the post office, government centers, schools, and the workplace? What about national identification cards with a smart chip that will have your personal information that lets law enforcement know that you are here legally?

These are but a few of the questions that should be debated by a free people. It all comes down to people, individuals at the local level, assessing their vulnerabil-ities, identifying the potential threat, and deciding what steps to take. Southwest Florida will be successful in this endeavor as long as the government, private sec-tor, and its citizens continue to be involved in the process and look at this issue using an interdisciplinary approach.

Airports:
State-of-the-Art Security Systems

"We will not tire. We will not falter. We will not fail."

—President George Bush

Introduction

On 9/11 the safety zone of citizens of the United States of America collapsed. The mind-set of the country changed forever. In order to make our citizens safe, our country was forced to modify, improve and execute numerous security systems. Airports were an instrumental part of these changes. In the dark days immediately after the tragedy, many experts wondered if the airline industry would survive (Hansen, 2002).

But recover we did. Airline and government officials worked diligently to provide our citizens with state-of-the-art airport security systems. On a national level, legislation was enacted, and new security was implemented. Two months after 9/11, President George Bush signed the landmark Aviation and Transportation Security Act. Under this law, the Federal government is responsible for performing most airport security duties. Key components of the Act include: 1) establishment of the Transportation Security Administration (TSA), and 2) a mandate that the TSA hire and train all screeners and other security personnel (Hansen, 2002).

The Civil Air Patrol

The Civil Air Patrol (CAP) is instrumental to implementing airport security legislation. The CAP is an official auxiliary of the United States Air Force. It operates under the authority of the Air Force Homeland Security. Along with providing security for the Olympics and the National Aeronautics and Space Administration launch sites, the CAP assisted with post 9/11 security measures.

The CAP is responsible for providing airborne reconnaissance and imagery, disaster and damage assessment, airborne transportation of personnel, equipment and critical supplies, and multi-layered communication support. In addition, the CAP has the capability of providing manpower for emergency operation centers, search and rescue teams, and ground support teams. Citizens of the United States of America can be comforted with the knowledge that the CAP has the technology to safely and cost effectively secure a major city or resource in less than two hours ("Civil Air Patrol Online," n.d.).

SEAL Act

In an effort to strengthen our nation's ability to prevent terrorist attacks, Congressman Edward Markey, a representative from Massachusetts' 7th District, updated the SEAL Act. Relevant sections of the updated Act include:

- Air cargo on passenger aircraft: The same equipment, technology and personnel screening passenger baggage will be used to screen air cargo on passenger aircrafts.

- Federal Air Marshals: Federal Air Marshals are required to be present on charter flights. All foreign flights must have a Federal Air Marshal or an equivalent officer of the government of the foreign country on board.

- Communication systems: Flight attendants are provided with a system for discreet, secure, hands-free, wireless method of communication with the pilots.

- Flight attendant training: Flight attendants are required to attend both classroom and hands-on self-defense training.

- Comprehensive pre-flight screening: Improved training for pre-flight screeners is required. Flight attendants are trained on how to properly conduct a pre-flight cabin search.

- Airport perimeters: Improved control over access to the secured area of all airports is required.

- Background checks for airport employees: All airport employees are subjected to a Social Security check and a check against all terrorist watch lists.

- Screening of airport employees: All airport employees are screened for metallic objects and their personal bags are inspected for chemical, biological or nuclear materials.

- Cockpit doors: Cockpit doors are to be locked and the wall surrounding the cockpit door is sufficient to secure the cockpit. ("Dogged Determination," 2005)

Southwest Florida Airports

Southwest Florida airports are among the busiest passenger and cargo airports in the nation (Robert M. Ball, Executive Director SW Florida International Airport, personal communication, July 14, 2005). Along with implementing the national legislation, Southwest Florida airports have enacted security systems that are unique to the region.

Southwest Florida International Airport

In July 1998, the Southwest Florida International Airport (RSW) began to implement a major expansion plan. After 9/11, many airports in the United States elected to halt their expansion. However RSW charged ahead. Over half of the money budgeted for design change was allotted directly to security. For example, the overall design was modified in order to create three separate four-lane security checkpoints with room for a fifth lane. RSW is the first new terminal in the United States designed with an in-line screening system. The lower level has a receiving dock where all shipments for terminal tenants will be screened through an Explosive Detection Screening (EDS). Robert Ball, Executive Director of RSW notes,

> We adjusted the budget for the project without impacting airline rates and charges. We're paying for it with passenger facility charge income, reserve finds, and transfers from other projects. It is important to see the improvement. We not only want to give comfort to our passengers and airport employees. We are most concerned with their security. (Robert Ball, personal communication, July 14, 2005)

Miami International Airport

After 9/11, screening of airline passengers intensified. Although this was a necessary security measure, it resulted in lengthy and often inconvenient wait-times. To counter this problem, Miami International Airport (MIA) will be implementing a state-of-the-art screening process. By spring 2006, an automated baggage screening system will be installed in the new South and North terminals. The process involves passengers checking their bags onto an automated conveyer belt. The conveyer belt will then transport the bags through explosive detection machines and move them on to the loading ramp. This system will eliminate hassle and save time for our passengers. It does away with a step so passengers wait less time with their bags. The Tampa and Jacksonville airports currently have this system in operation.

Conclusion

Our safety zone has reformed. We are stronger and more aware of our surroundings. The efforts made to enhance the safety of our citizens will only continue to be fortified. The landmark aviation and Transportation Security Act offers us reforms that instill confidence in our air transportation systems. Citizens of Southwest Florida are protected by airport security systems that are unique to the area.

Temples:
New Approaches to Security

"Intolerance lies at the core of evil. Not the intolerance that results from any threat or danger. But intolerance of another being who dares to exist. It is so deep within us, because every human being secretly desires the entire universe to himself. Our only way out is to learn compassion without cause. To care for each other simply because that 'other' exists.."

—Rabbi Menachem Mendle

Since 9/11 temples around the country have tried several new approaches that have increased security in general (Lori Cohen, Executive Director, Temple Shalom of Naples, personal communication, July 19, 2005). The style of security varies among temples from big cities to rural areas. The commonality is the buildings are locked when the temple is not open for worship. During regular business hours, the doors are locked, and a person must identify him-herself before entering. This can be done with a doorbell, security camera or volunteer sitting at the door. They strive to maintain a comfortable feeling. Even with the doors closed, they try to be as welcoming as possible. The members have become used to the added security and have come to appreciate this comfort level. People are not disappointed by the fact that the doors must be closed. They understand this is in response to the state of our world.

Temples are becoming more proactive. Personnel are well versed in security procedures. The staff and volunteers receive suspicious behavior training from the sheriff's department. They learn the specifics that alert them to identify potential trouble. They are then taught what to do until the authorities arrive. Communication is enhanced within the facilities. In big cities, many temples have on-site security. Other temples employ uniformed officers. Lori Cohen,

Executive Director of Temple Shalom in Naples states, "Incidents should be avoided" (personal communication, July 19, 2005).

Collier County Schools: A Proactive Security Leader

"There is a lot of talk now about metal detectors and gun control. Both are good things. But they are no more a solution than forks and spoons are a solution to world hunger."

—Anna Quinlan

Introduction

Americans once considered our learning institutions to be sanctuaries—places where our young children went to learn. We gave little thought to how safe they were from threats of outside violence. Gifted teachers were certainly equipped to handle any disruption that occurred inside the classroom walls. However, since 9/11, the perception of school security has changed.

It is not only the reaction from external terrorist activities, such as the strikes on New York City, Pennsylvania and Washington D.C. that worries educators. It is the well-planned attacks that come from within the school walls. For example, the tragic incidence at Columbine High School shook our country and our world. The Columbine incident lasted 46 minutes and left 15 dead ("Columbine High School Massacre," n.d.). The terrorist activity was well thought-out and meticuliously planned. And it was conducted by students of that very school.

Another tragic attack from within occurred a continent away in Beslan, Russia. Beslan is 19 miles (30 km) north of Vladikavkaz in southern Russia. It borders the troubled Russian republic of Chechnya. On September 1, 2004, terrorists entered and took-down a school in this city. After two days, amid explosions and shootings, the siege came to an end. Three hundred and thirty-six people were left dead—about half of whom were children. Former hostages told authorities that the terrorists had weapons and explosives that were hidden in the school before the siege ("How did Terrorists Attack the School at Beslan, Russia?" n.d.). Not only was this a horrific act. It also raised an alarming question: How did bombs and weapons get into the school before the terrorists?

Collier County Schools: District 6

The Collier County Schools are prepared to prevent such atrocities. The district leads the way in ensuring Florida will limit the vulnerability to terrorist threats and activities. In relation to other regions of Florida and the nation as a whole, the school district is at an advanced level of preparedness. In addition, it serves as a national model for other regions of the United States. Many districts in Florida and several out of state school districts have copied the Emergency Preparedness guide for class rooms including, Missouri, Delaware and North Carolina (Ed Messer, Safety and Security, Collier County Schools, personal communication, July 15, 2005).

There is no secret to the success of Collier County School District's rapid implementation of strengthening terrorism preparedness. At the heart of this success is 1) partnering of all regional agencies to tackle the threat and emergency crisis as one cohesive unit, 2) continuously training and cross-training county district employees, and 3) continuously seeking technology improvements and upgrades to make the schools a safer place for students and employees.

School Districts Partnerships

When there is an eminent threat on a school campus in the district, the old method of letting one agency get approval, waiting for another agency to complete a task, and then when the coast is clear, moving slowly toward the terrorist threat is a thing of the past. The Collier County District School Board is involved in a partnership with seven regional agencies. They are: 1) the Sheriff's Office, 2) Regional Domestic Security Task Force, 3) Collier County Health Department, 4) the local community based mental health agency, 5) local government, 6) Collier County emergency Management, and 7) North Naples Fire and Rescue District and the seven other fire districts also provide NIMS training ("Emergency Response and Crisis Management Grant Application," n.d.) Each partner has a specific set of roles and responsibilities. Each one is an integral part of a team that strengthens school security.

The Collier County Sheriff's Office is an ongoing partner with school preparedness and emergency response procedures for all Collier County schools. It is the key partner in establishing and coordinating rapid, concise and effective multi-agency emergency response to each campus in the district. In the quest to continue and update the plan, this office provides preplanning, tactical information and ground command coordination.

The Regional Domestic Security Task Force and Collier County Schools are partners in the emergency responses and crisis management planning. They operate under the direction of the district superintendent and the task force chairs. The Collier County school system serves as the educational chair of the Region 6 Domestic Security Task Force. Information and policy updates are regularly reviewed and acted upon.

The Collier County Health Department meets regularly and plans and prepares in accordance with the Collier County Schools' staff threat scenarios and emergency response protocols. This is ongoing and stays current with the changing events that may threaten the schools in Collier County.

The David Lawrence Mental Health Center is a partner in the emergency planning for mental health professionals. In the event of a crisis, it assists the Collier County School District. The David Lawrence Mental Health Center employs the district's mental health caregivers. In the event of a trauma, it has in place plans to mitigate mental health issues for both students and staff.

The Collier County Government is a continuing partner with the Collier County Schools on implementing and preplanning for emergencies. The county government works hand-in-hand with top administration and department heads on continued crises planning and mitigation. The combined efforts and asset management projections are continuous and done to improve currently in-place and future plans.

Collier County Emergency Management works regularly with Collier County Schools on crisis management, preplanning, mitigation, and recovery. From weather emergencies to man-made threats or catastrophes, emergency management is a continuous partner in improving the plan.

The North Naples Fire and Rescue District is Collier County School's key partner in developing and compiling information for data integration for all responding fire districts in Collier County. North Naples Fire District is also the train-the-trainer authority for the grant-developed security training. North Naples Fire Department has been and will continue to be the lead fire partner for Collier County Schools. The goal is to insure continuous improvement of the plan.

Since the terrible acts of 9/11, Columbine and Beslan, the philosophy of how to eliminate the danger of an act of terrorism has changed. The eminent danger will be eliminated in a very short period of time. "It will be treated like a fire" indicated Ed Messer (Ed Messer, Safety and Security, Collier County Schools, personal communication, July 15, 2005). Mr. Messer goes on to explain that a situation like Columbine or Beslan will never happen in Collier County schools. Authorities will attack the problem directly at its source. The situation will be over in a matter of minutes instead of hours or days. Collier County's Emergency Forces reaction to school incidents will be concise, immediate and effective.

Alert Levels

Working together with the created partnership, the school district follows a specific set of procedures that are incorporated into site-specific plans developed at each school. Each school has a specific committee that devotes itself to this task. These procedures are to be followed in each of the terrorist threat-level conditions established by the Department of Homeland Security ("The District School Board of Collier County," 2005).

Depending on the nature of the over-all threat to the nation, the Department of Homeland Security has five threat conditions. The most critical conditions occur at Threat Condition Severe (Red). To assist in defining the specific responses to be implemented at Treat Condition Severe (Red), the local Region 6 Domestic Security Task Force will issue an alert level that is specific to the region and Collier County. These threat levels will determine which procedures the District School Board of Collier County will use ("The District School Board of Collier County," 2005). The threat levels are as follows:

Threat Level 1—Credible Threat to Collier County and Threat Level 2—Credible Threat to Region 6: Schools will be closed. The District Communications Office and Information Office will make announcements. If these announcements are made during a school day, the superintendent will determine the appropriate time to release the students. When they are released, students will only be released to an authorized parent. If the Threat Levels 1 or 2 are declared before a school day starts, the superintendent will announce the closure of the schools. School administrators will ensure that their campuses are secure. Then all buildings will be closed and locked. Before reopening and allowing students and staff to return to school, administrators in coordination with the Youth Relations Deputy assigned to that school will inspect the campus to ensure that it is safe.

Threat Level 3—Credible Threat to Florida: Schools will remain open. Implementation of all actions required at lower threat conditions and threat levels will occur. Escorts will be provided to all campus visitors. The school administration and the Assistant Superintendent will evaluate all after-school activities. It will then be determined whether or not to cancel the activity. All school activity travel will be canceled. Barriers will be placed and doors locked in critical areas such as electrical rooms, air handlers and chemical storage areas. As in everyday procedures, a single-entry and single-exit control point for vehicle and pedestrian traffic will be established. A remote location will be designated for package delivery and communication to carriers. If parking spaces are located within 300 hundred feet of the endangered area, they will be restricted. Internal communication plans will be tested. All escort staff and control point staff will be equipped with 2-way communication devices. The Youth Relations Deputy will be reassigned by the law enforcement agency. A procedure for parent pickup with access restrictions will be established.

Threat level 4—Credible Threat to the United States: Schools will remain open. The implementation of all actions required at lower threat conditions and threat levels will be made. It will be verified that there is a 72 hours supply of food and schools are stocked with first aid and medical supplies. The fuel levels will be topped off for generators and school vehicles. A process to respond to parent inquiries and to dispel any rumors in accordance with the information released from the District Information and Communication Office will be established. The need for any after school activities and activity travel will be evaluated. The administration will then make a decision whether or not to cancel school. In order to prevent theft, tampering or destruction, buildings, unused rooms, storage areas, equipment and vehicles will be secured.

Threat Level 5—No Credible Threat—Country at War: Schools will remain open. The implementation of all actions required at lower threat conditions and threat levels will be made. The Youth Relations Deputy will increase his or her patrol on campus. The monitoring of world news events will be carried out by partner agencies and the Collier County School District. Any concerns on campus will be communicated to the Youth Relations Deputy. Any suspicious packages and individuals will be reported to the Sheriff's Department. All locking systems and security barriers such as fencing will be inspected for operability. Emergency preparedness information will be provided to all Collier County School District employees. All employees will adhere to travel guidelines.

Background Checks

Something that most of us take for granted is the speed and efficiency that technology contributes to our daily lives. The District School Board of Collier County does not take technology for granted. Board members see technology as a tool that can be used to make the students, teachers and employees of Collier County schools safer. Newer technology is always being researched and evaluated. Currently, a new system to track, identify and provide background checks is being examined by the School Board of Collier County and Department of Security and Environmental Management (Ed Messer, Director of Safety and Security, Collier County Schools, personal communication, July 15, 2005).

This rapid identification and tracking system processes visitors into buildings by taking their picture, compiling personal background information, storing it into a software system and printing a temporary identification badge. In a matter of seconds, this system will be able to access law enforcement databases such as sex offender databases, violent criminal databases and FBI most wanted databases. For example, if a convicted pedophile were to try to gain access to a campus, he would have to present his drivers license. The license barcode would then be swiped along the scanner. The scanner would then access these databases through the Internet. The result of the background check would be processed and returned to the school employee before the individual finished signing his name and date. Access to the school campus would be refused.

Each school is assigned a Student Relations Deputy. This law enforcement officer is provided at no cost to the school by the Collier County Sheriff's Department. If a terrorism attack or threat occurs at that school, the Sheriff's Department can quickly reassign the deputy to best suit the situation at hand.

Red and Green Folder

An important and very effective tool that is at the disposal of The District School Board of Collier County is called *The Red and Green Folder*. This folder contains procedures for each threat level as well as safety procedures for Fire/Explosion, Intruder on Campus, Major Student Disruption, Severe Weather, and Weapons or Guns on Campus.

Safety Committee

Along with the above described procedures, each school has a safety committee. This committee is comprised of teachers of that respective school. They know the physical layout of the campus as well as the policies and procedures of the Collier County School District. Using their expertise, they are able to make informed security decisions for their school. By using the School District's best practices, they create policies and plans tailored to that particular school.

Conclusion

When it comes to safety and security, the Collier County School District is one of the most proactive school districts in the country. Success does not lead to complacency. By partnering with district agencies, utilizing security technologies and being in a continuous state of improvement, the district is a model for other school districts throughout the country.

Practical Application

This case study outlines numerous governmental changes that work to protect the citizens of Southwest Florida from acts of terrorism. It also describes in detail procedures that Southwest Florida first responders use in the wake of a terrorist attack. Southwest Florida is not alone in improving intelligence and security aimed at combating terrorism. Using the case questions as a guide, examine the security in your local community. What post-9/11 improvements were made? How have these improvements increased security in your area?

Next, develop your own suggestions for a terrorist alert system. Build upon the current national alert system—adapt it for your unique area. Give examples as to how it will work in various venues such as schools, hospitals, airports and local targets. Describe the specifics of your new alert system. Follow this description with statistical and graphical information that will better define the alert system's potential to increase the security in your area.

Case Questions

1. What is/are your local hospital(s), terrorism response plan(s)?

2. What is your local government doing to protect citizens from a terrorist attack?

3. What alert systems are used in your community?

4. Is your local community a travel destination? If yes, what safeguards, both pre-and post-9/11 are in place to protect the citizens in your area?

5. Are you in an area that requires increased highway security? If yes, what security measures are in place to protect your infrastructure?

6. First responders play a key role in the safety of local citizens. What is the security plan of your local first responders? Include firefighters, EMTs, paramedics and SWAT teams.

7. How are your schools protected against acts of terrorism?

8. How are your utilities protected against acts of terrorism?

9. What can you, as a private citizen, do to prepare for a terrorist attack?

10. What can you do to increase your community's awareness of security in your area?

11. What can you do to participate in your community's security efforts?

An Interdisciplinary Perspective: Reflections

"One of the greatest discoveries a man makes, one of his great surprises, is to find he can do what he was afraid he couldn't do."

—Henry Ford

It is important for one to recognize how goals and abilities are obtained. Our case study was a vast journey, one that deserves everlasting recognition from each of us. Interdisciplinary studies prepares us with skills we need to succeed in a project of this magnitude. We leap over the bar of challenges in ways we never before even dreamed about.

Each class in the interdisciplinary studies program integrates concepts and skills from several disciplines. Thus, as students, we have the ability to play diverse roles. Those of us who thought we would never make good leaders have new perspectives on leadership and the roles we play. Our critical thinking skills are expanded in ways we never thought possible. We learn to strengthen our abilities to look far beyond the obvious. Our research and writing abilities are incorporated in every project we do, which makes us more creative, mature, and distinguished writers. We have communication skills that expand both our oral and electronic abilities. We understand the importance of communicating effectively. Thus, we have the ability to birth our ideas in a creative and progressive manner.

As interdisciplinary students, we foster the ability to achieve diverse perspectives and harmonize these perspectives. We are able to look upon social and ethical issues without bias. We enlarge our views with creative and unconventional thinking. And we do this with a high measure of cognitive development.

We learn to work effectively with others, recognizing the meaning of a team. We are able to work through obstacles and understand the existence of nonconformity. We understand that by maintaining curiosity and the desire to go beyond what is expected, we do not have to accept failure. This gives us the ability to produce Southwest Florida's Plan to Combat Terrorism: An Interdisciplinary Perspective.

We are sincerely grateful for International College's interdisciplinary studies program and give kudos to our professor, Dr. Judith Kolva, who guided us, supported us, encouraged us and challenged us. We move on from the interdisciplinary studies program proud and prepared to proclaim our achievements.

References

America's waterway watch. (n.d.). Retrieved August 24, 2005, from http://americaswaterwaywatch.org/

Beiner, R. (2004). The criminology of terrorism: Theories and models. Retrieved June 24, 2005, from http://faculty.ncwc.edu/toconnor/429/429lect02.htm

Bonita Springs Utilities, Inc. (2004). Annual Report.

Boxleitner, G. (2004). Lee takes part in training exercises: EMT's prepare for various nightmare scenarios. The News-Press. Retrieved June 23, 2005, from Infoweb.

Boxleitner, G. (2005). Division plans forward thinking. The News-Press. Retrieved July 12, 2005, from Infoweb.

Carafano, J. (n.d.). Top homeland security priorities for the next four years. Retrieved August 22, 2005, from http://www.heritage.org/Research/HomelandDefense/em955.cfm

Citizen Corps. (n.d.). Council profiles and resources. Retrieved July 4, 2005, from http://www.citizencorps.gov/

Civil Air Patrol online. (n.d.). Retrieved July 12, 2005, from http://www.cap.gov/

Collier County Comprehensive Emergency Management Plan. (2005). Retrieved June 14, 2005, from http://collierem.org/PDF/ENTRY.htm

Collier County Emergency Management. (n.d.). Community emergency response teams. Retrieved July 4, 2005, from http://www.collierem.org/

Collier County Sheriff's Office. (n.d.). Retrieved July 11, 2005, from http://www.colliersheriff.org/aboutus/sheriff/bio.stm

Columbine High School massacre. (n.d.). Retrieved July 2, 2005, from http://en.wikipedia.org/wiki/Columbine_High_School_Massacre

Coon, D. (2004). Introduction to psychology. Belmont, CA: Wadsworth/Thompson Learning.

Copeland, C. & Cody, B. (2005). Terrorism and security issues facing the water infrastructure sector. CRS Report for Congress. Retrieved June 16, 2005, from http://www.fas.org/sgp/crs/terror/RL32189.pdf

Council on Foreign Relations. (n.d.). Terrorism: question and answer. Retrieved June 10, 2005, from http://cfrterrorism.org/security/police.html

Council on Foreign Relations. (2004). Suicide terror: Was 9/11 something new? Retrieved June 14, 2005, from http://www.cfrterrorism.org/terrorism/suicide2.html

Davies, F. (2005). Domestic terrorism still a threat. Retrieved June 18, 2005, from Infotrac.

Department of Homeland Security. (n.d. a). Homeland security secretary Michael Chertoff announces six-point agenda for department of homeland security. Retrieved July 16, 2005, from http://www.dhs.gov

Department of Homeland Security. (n.d. b). Fact sheet: a better prepared America: a year in review. Retrieved July 12, 2005, from http://www.dhs.gov/dhspublic/display?theme=43&content=3854&print=true

Department of Homeland Security. (n.d. c). Three key steps that individuals and families should take to be properly prepared for unexpected emergencies. Retrieved July 12, 2005, from http://www.dhs.gov/dhspublic/display?theme=14&content=462&print=true

Department of Homeland Security. (n.d. d). Emergencies & disasters. Retrieved July 11, 2005, from http://www.dhs.gov/dhspublic/index.jsp

Dipietre, J. (2005). Governor Bush and executive command staff participate in annual homeland security exercise. Retrieved July 11, 2005, from www.floridadisaster.org/documents/39027619.pdf

Dogged determination. (2005). Retrieved July 5, 2005, from LexisNexis.

Eggen, D. E. & Wilson, S. (2005). Suicide bombs potent tools of terrorists. Retrieved July 17, 2005, from http://www.washingtonpost.com/wp-dyn/content/article/2005/07/16/AR2005071601363.html

Emergency response and crisis management grant application, section XII. partner agreements. (n.d.). Retrieved July 21, 2005, from http://www.ed.gov/fund/grant/apply/grantapps/2004/84184e.html

Emery, G.J. (2004). History of terrorism: Timeline of terrorist acts. Retrieved July 22, 2005, from http://www.crimsonbird.com/terrorism/timeline.htm

FAIR. (2005). Retrieved June 18, 2005, from http:fairus.org/site/PageServer?Pagename=research_researchlist4847

Florida Department of Law Enforcement and State Division of Emergency Management. (2001). Strengthening domestic security in Florida. Retrieved July 11, 2005, from http://www.fdle.state.fl.us/

Florida Department of Transportation. (2004). Retrieved June 20, 2005, from http://www.dot.state.fl.us/

Freedom fighter. (2005). Retrieved July 18, 2005, from http://en.wikipedia.org/wiki/Freedom_fighter

Galak, M. (2005). The psychopathology of terrorism. Retrieved June 18, 2005, from Infotrac.

German, M. (2005, June 6). Domestic terrorism: The threat from within. The Washington Post.

Goodlette, J. D. (2004). Florida domestic security: Report by the Coordinating Committee on Public Security. Tallahassee, FL: Florida House of Representatives.

Governors office. (2001). Governor Bush signs executive order related to domestic security issues in Florida. Retrieved July 12, 2005, from www.doh.state.fl.us/terrorism/pressrelease/domestic security RLS.pdf

Hall, M. (2005, March 11). EMS lacks terrorism training, equipment. USA Today. Retrieved May 10, 2005, from http://www.usatoday.com/news/nation/2005-03-10-ems-lax-x.htm

Harmon, C.C. (2001). Terrorism today. Portland, OR: Frank Cass Publishers.

Hanson, B. (2002). Future of the Airline Industry. Retrieved July 12, 2005 from CQ Researcher.

Hebert, R. (2001). A brief discussion of water securities issues following the September 11, 2001 terrorist attacks. Retrieved June 15, 2005, from http://ncppp.org/inthenews/waterdiscussion.html

Hansen, B. (2002) Future of The Airline Industry, Volume 12, Number 24. Retrieved July 12, 2005 from CQ Researcher.

Highway Information Sharing and Analysis Center. (2005). *The American Trucking Industry's Anti-Terrorism Action Plan* Retrieved July 3, 2005, from https://www.highwayisac.org/

Homeland Security presidential directive/Hspd-7. (2003). Retrieved July 2, 2005, from http://www.whitehouse.gov/news/releases/2003/12/print/20031217-5.html

How did terrorists attack the school at Beslan, Russia? KeysToSaferSchools.com, Retrieved July 7, 2005, from http://www.keystosaferschools.com/russia shoolhostagesupdate.htm

Hudson, R. (1999). *The sociology and psychology of terrorism: Who becomes a terrorist and why?* Retrieved June 4, 2005, from http://www.fas.org/irp/threat/frd.html

Huntington, S. P. (1996). *The clash of civilizations: Remaking of world order.* New York: Touchstone.

Husty, D. (2002). Three men released after perceived terror plot. *The News-Press.* Retrieved July 12, 2005, from Infoweb.

Husty, D. (2004). Hunter defends actions on Alley. *The News-Press.* Retrieved July 12, 2005, from Infoweb.

Inside the FBI: Eco-Terrorism. (2002). *The Washington Post Company* Retrieved June 14, 2005, from http://discuss.washingtonpost.com/wp-srv/zforum/02/fbi0227.htm

Kegley, C. W. & Raymond, G. A. (2005). *The global future.* Belmont, CA: Wadsworth/Thomson Learning.

Kobach, K. (2004). State and local authority to enforce immigration law: An unified approach for stopping terrorists. Retrieved July 11, 2005, from http://www.cis.org/articles/2004/back604.html

Ku Klux Klan. (2005). Retrieved June 30, 2005 from http://en.wikipedia.org/wiki/Ku_Klux_Klan

Kushner, H. W. (1998). *Terrorism in America: A structured approach to understanding the terrorist threat.* Springfield, IL: Charles C. Thomas Publishers Ltd.

Left, S. & Oliver, M. (2005). 38 Dead in London Blasts, *The Guardian Unlimited.* Retrieved July 16, 2005, from http://www.guardian.co.uk/transport/Story/0,1523084,00.html

Love, M. C. (2003). *Beyond sovereignty.* Belmont, CA: Wadsworth/Thomson Learning.

Mansfield, D. (2005). Security breach at nuclear plant. Retrieved June 22, 2005, from http://www.cbsnews.com/stories/2005/06/20/national/main703076.shtml?CMP=ILC-SearchStories

McVeigh sentenced to death in federal bombing. (1997). Retrieved June 16, 2005, from http://encarta.msn.com/sidebar_762512236/McVeigh_Sentenced_to_Death_in_Federal_Bombing.html

Mitch, F. (2004). Four dots American intelligence failed to connect. *Time Canada (vol. 163, issue 17).* Retrieved June 6, 2005, from Ebsco Host.

Moghaddam, F.M. & Marsella, A.J. (Eds.). (2004). *Understanding Terrorism.* Washington, DC: American Psychological Association.

Mylroie, L. (1995). *The world trade center bombing: Who is Ramzi Yousef? And why it matters.* Retrieved June 30, 2005, from http://www.fas.org/irp/world/iraq/956-tni.htm

Naples Community Hospital. (2002). *Terrorism Incident Report.*

O'Day, A. (2004). *Dimensions of terrorism.* Aldershot Hants, England: Ashgate Publishing Ltd.

Operation on guard. (n.d.). Retrieved August 22, 2005, from http://www.fdle.state.fl.us/alerts/2002/on_guard.html

Orange County Sheriff's Office. (2005). Retrieved July 11, 2005, from http://www.ocso.com/

Petri, T. (2005). *Statement at Hearing on Background Check Process for Truckers' Hazmat Endorsements: U.S. House Committee on Transportation and Infrastructure.* Retrieved June 13, 2005, from http://www.house.gov/trans portation/press/press2005/release59.html

Price, D.A. (2002). Securing Our Nation's Highway System. *Public Roads, September/October 66*(2).

Ready.Gov U.S. Department of Homeland Security. (n.d.). Retrieved August 12, 2005, from www.ready.gov

Reign of terror. (n.d.). Retrieved June 30, 2005 from http://www.historywiz.com/terror.htm

Ruane, D. (2002, September 14). Response, investigation into incident pass test. *The News-Press.* Retrieved July 12, 2005, from Infoweb

Stacy, M. (2005). *Witness: USF shunned professor's think tank when terrorist ties emerged.* Retrieved June 13, 2005, from http://www.tcpalm.com/tcp/home/article/0,1651, TCP_996_3852291,00.html

Stoessinger, J. G. (2005). *Why nations go to war.* Belmont, CA: Wadsworth/Thomson Learning.

Terrorism. (2005). Retrieved July 17, 2005, from http://encarta.msn.com/encyclopedia_761564344_2/Terrorism.html

The Blue Ribbon Panel on Bridge and Tunnel Security. (2003). *Recommendations for Bridge and Tunnel Security.* Retrieved July 16, 2005, from http://www.fwha.dot.gov/bridge/security/brptoc.htm

The Bombing. (1996). Retrieved July 24, 2005, from http://www.cnn.com/US/OKC/bombing.html

The District School Board of Collier County. (2005). Terrorism preparedness for Schools: Alert levels guide and recommendations.

The World Trade Center bombing. (2005). Retrieved June 30, 2005 from http://www.adl.org/learn/jttf/wtcb_jttf.asp

United States Department of Justice. (n.d.). *Dispelling some of the major myths about the USA PATRIOT Act*. Retrieved July 16, 2005, from http://www.lifeandliberty.gov/subs/u_myths.htm

Valine, K. (2001). Muslim leaders get FDLE's ear. *Sarasota Herald Tribune*, p. B1, C1.

Volpe Center highlights-January/February (2003). *Focus*. Retrieved July 16, 2005, from http://www.volpe.dot.gov/infosrc/highlts/03/janfeb/d_focus.html

What is terrorism? (n.d.). Retrieved June 13, 2005, from http://www.brevard county.us/EOC/haz_terrorism.cfm

Wipf, P. (2002). *Immigration before and after*. Retrieved June 13, 2005, from http://immigration.about.com/library/weekly

978-0-595-40404-9
0-595-40404-9